STRANGERS
IN THE
SENATE

Strangers in the Senate

Politics and the New Revolution of Women in America

Senator Barbara Boxer

with

Nicole Boxer

National
Press
Books

Washington, D.C.

Library of Congress Cataloging-in-Publication Data

Boxer, Barbara, 1940-
Strangers in the Senate: politics and the new revolution of women in America
by Barbara Boxer and Nicole Boxer:
foreword by Hillary Rodham Clinton.
256 pp., 156 x 22.5 cm.
Includes index.
ISBN 1-882605-06-3: $23.95
1. Women in politics—United States.
2. Women legislators—United States.
3. Sex discrimination against women—United States.
4. Women—United States—social conditions.
I. Boxer, Nicole, 1967-
II. Title.

HQ1391.U5B69 1993	93-36098
320'.082—dc20	CIP

PRINTED IN THE UNITED STATES OF AMERICA

1 2 3 4 5 6 7 8 9 10

For my family—

whose love gives me courage.

Acknowledgments

I wish to thank:

Sam Chapman, Gina Pennestri and my staff—whose dedication to the people is unquestioned;

Jackie de Nevers—whose friendship and common sense have guided me since 1975;

John Burton and George Miller—who taught me never to walk away from the truth;

Marilyn Bergman—without whom I never would have run for the U.S. Senate;

and the women of the United States Senate—past, present and future.

Contents

Beforeword

The television announcer's voice came in clearly over the noise and excitement of the crowd: "The California U.S. Senate race is still too close to call."

Voices hushed as the mass of bodies crowded around the 20-inch tube that was their link to reality. It was this media box that would let them know if their hours of licking envelopes, soliciting contributions and walking door to door had been worth it, that would tell them if the anti-war movement was indeed only a small group of dissidents in California, or a real, thriving, growing constituency that would let the world know on this election day that they wanted out of the fruitless and devastating war in Vietnam.

In the middle of the crowd in campaign headquarters, with the race too close to call, stood Carol Wynn. At five feet three, with shining black hair and blue eyes—"like Elizabeth Taylor's," her mother would say—Carol could have been the attractive woman selling soap, cereal, or sewing machines in a myriad of television commercials. But Carol Wynn wanted to be a U.S. Senator from the most populous state in the union, a state which, by electing her, would be saying, "End this unpopular and needless war and end it now."

Carol had been elected the most popular girl in her high school, and she looked ten years younger than her 37 years—something that drove Ted Hunter, her campaign manager, crazy. "For God's sake, Carol, do something with you hair—add a little gray or something," he'd plead.

But Carol wouldn't change her hair or her clothes or anything else. Newspaper photos caught her in T-shirt and jeans walking along Point Reyes National Seashore with her eight-year-old daughter. TV cameramen interviewed her at home with an apron on and baking soda in her hair. "God, is this a Senator?" moaned an anguished Ted when he saw the pictures.

But when Carol Wynn spoke, it didn't matter what she looked like, because the audience was caught by her voice. Her words were the words of a secure and intelligent candidate—a caring and humane leader. That's why the race was so close. That's why she was in it at all.

Her opponent, Gary Lansing III, had outspent Carol three to one. All the major corporations endorsed him, and he strutted around in his three-piece pin-striped suit with an air of confidence, citing his military record and sporting his beautiful wife on his arm. She looked as she did in all his campaign brochures—adoring and contented. In fact, she was his secret weapon. "Gary," she would tell a charmed press corps, "is so chivalrous that it simply breaks his heart to run against a woman. But he feels that for the sake of our state and our country—not to mention Ms. Wynn's daughter—that he simply has to win!" Her wifely speech proved to be so popular that it was even made into a television commercial aimed at daytime soap-opera watchers.

Now Carol looked at the nervous, anxious faces on the people hovering around the TV. Exhausted, she nonetheless made a tremendous effort to pull herself together and climbed to the podium to address her campaign workers. Immediately, there was silence.

"My beautiful people," she began, "—and tonight you are mine, you are a part of me—six months we have followed a path together. I was placed on that path by you and you have guided me along it. It has been difficult, and sometimes hazardous, but because of you,

I found my way. And whatever happens tonight, I'll continue to find my way."

"We'll win tonight, Carol!" cried the voices from the crowd.

"We will win, dear friends," she continued in a quiet tone, "only when we no longer send our children to die in a war we cannot understand, let alone win. Win or lose tonight, my heart will only be free when we know that loyal young men who lie in hospitals all over this country no longer have to weep for those who are coming to lie in the beds next to them. And I pledge to you tonight, with all my strength, that we will win! Either from the floor of the Senate or the steps of the Capitol, we will be heard!"

Applause rang through the headquarters. Tears welled up. Hands reached out for other hands.

"It is going to be a long night for us," said Carol. "We won't know the results of our race until the morning hours. I'm going home to be with my daughter and my mother and you should all go home to be with your loved ones. I will be here tomorrow morning at ten a.m. no matter what the results, and I will want to be with all of you. Can I count on that?"

A deafening "yes" came back to her.

Carol grabbed her purse and raincoat and walked among all the familiar and worried faces, touching hands, kissing cheeks; she left with Ted guiding her through the crowd. Outside, the rain was beating down. Carol lifted her face to welcome the cool drops of rain. Northern California weather is so sensible, she thought; six months of sun, six months of rain.

"God, Carol, all we need is a cold for your victory speech," said Ted as he thrust an umbrella over her head. "Now please get in under this umbrella."

—from an unfinished, unpublished novel written by Barbara Boxer in 1973, 20 years before she was sworn in as a United States Senator from California

Foreword

Throughout American history, women have left an indelible imprint on the political landscape. As unsung activists, courageous pioneers and more recently as elected officials, women have overcome once insurmountable odds to shape political attitudes and transform the national agenda.

From Abigail Adams to Elizabeth Cady Stanton to Eleanor Roosevelt to Shirley Chisholm to Geraldine Ferraro to Barbara Boxer, American women have been vanguards of societal reform since the 18th century. A vast array of issues bear their stamp: the abolition of slavery, women's suffrage, pay equity, child welfare, protections for the elderly, health care and education.

What do women add to political life? Brains, energy and dedication. But even more important, a compassion and sensitivity borne of their own life experiences—and a unique perspective on the government's role in helping people.

Not that women have ever been fully welcome in the political arena. First Lady Abigail Adams, a trusted (if unofficial) adviser to the nation's second President and a vocal critic of slavery, was mocked by many for her interest in the affairs of state. In the mid-19th century, reformer Elizabeth Cady Stanton's father briefly disinherited her because of her outspoken views on women's rights and religion. Activist Susan B. Anthony was arrested and fined $100 for voting—before women's suffrage had been established—in the 1872 Presidential election. First Lady

Eleanor Roosevelt was admonished in newspaper editorials, even before her husband was inaugurated in 1933, to keep her opinions to herself. And Geraldine Ferraro was scrutinized in the press more than any other Vice Presidential candidate in history when she ran on the Democratic ticket in 1984.

But progress, while slow, has come. Just in the last 20 years, the first woman elected governor in her own right took office in Connecticut. The first woman was appointed to the Supreme Court. The first woman was nominated for the Vice Presidency of the United States by a major party. In 1992, the so-called "Year of the Woman," more women than ever before were elected to office. Perhaps as important, women nowadays vote at a higher rate than men.

Seven women now grace the U.S. Senate, including the first African-American woman, Carol Moseley-Braun, a Democrat from Illinois. There are 47 women in the House of Representatives, about a quarter of whom are women of color. Women now occupy 22 percent of statewide offices and 20 percent of the seats in state legislatures. The mayors of 18 percent of our cities are women.

Before winning the right to vote or gaining elective offices, women who wanted to affect social change had to rely on the power of the pen, the power of speech, and the power of outside pressure groups—such as the temperance, suffrage and abolitionist movements organized by Elizabeth Cady Stanton and Susan B. Anthony in the 19th century. And what perseverance they showed! Thanks in large part to the courage and spirit of many visible and not-so-visible women, political isolation could only last so long.

Throughout their lives, Elizabeth Cady Stanton and Susan B. Anthony were no strangers to controversy, no strangers to hostility from their opponents. Yet for more than half a century they fought for their principles, paving the way for all women today.

While pressing for women's suffrage, Stanton and Anthony succeeded in winning historic legal reforms for women. In 1848, at Stanton's prodding, the New York legislature gave married women the right to hold property in their own names. Six years later, Stanton became the first woman ever to address the assembly—and she spoke about the legal disabilities afflicting women. In 1860, Anthony was instrumental in pushing for state legislation that gave women the right to retain their own earnings and sue in court.

Legal advances begot economic and political advances. Women sought equal pay for equal work and equal educational opportunities. Slowly but surely the tide began to turn. And finally, in 1917, the first woman ever to serve in Congress arrived on Capitol Hill. Pacifist and suffragist Jeannette Rankin was elected from Montana and cast the lone vote against U.S. involvement in World War I.

But no woman in American history influenced the political agenda as much as former First Lady Eleanor Roosevelt. Mrs. Roosevelt felt a duty to help society's neglected, and she made the underprivileged her special cause. She traveled to Puerto Rico to inspect conditions in the slums. She toured the back alleys of Washington in her Buick to learn about poverty in urban America. She showed up at Appalachian coal mines. She visited Indian reservations. And she went on the stump, campaigning for the New Deal with conviction and vigor.

She answered racial injustice by setting her own example of social morality. Once, at a meeting in Alabama, she was so discouraged to find the crowd segregated by race that she moved her chair in the middle of the aisle separating whites and blacks.

As a model of independent courage and power, Eleanor Roosevelt inspired millions of women to participate politically—a notion that only a few decades earlier had seemed unthinkable. One woman Mrs. Roosevelt deeply influenced was Crystal Fauset, who in 1938 became the first African-American woman elected to a state legislature. Acclaimed for her dedication to civil rights and her powerful oratory in the Pennsylvania assembly, Fauset tirelessly urged other women, particularly minority women, to get involved in politics.

Although more aware of their potential in the political arena, women remained largely on the fringes of power for several more decades. Thirty years after winning the right to vote, women had won some important political reforms, but they were still too few in number to reshape political institutions. More work, more participation, and more awareness were needed.

And all three came in waves in the late 1960s and 1970s. Slowly, women began to attract attention and to sway the nation's political agenda more directly. One of the most moving examples I can remember was Barbara Jordan's brilliant, eloquent speech during the Watergate hearings in 1974. Jordan, a Congresswoman from Texas, passionately extoled the Constitution while calling for the impeachment of President Nixon.

Women in government made a difference not only with powerful oratory, but with powerful deeds. Issues overlooked for years suddenly took on new importance. In 1973 Congress passed Title IX, landmark legislation that ensured equal funding for women at colleges and universities receiving federal aid. Laws were passed to assist women in business, the workplace, the medical world, and in the courts.

According to a survey of state legislators conducted by the Center for the American Woman and Politics at Rutgers University, the presence of women in the political arena led to an increase in legislation affecting children, the elderly, education, health care, and the environment— issues historically ignored by men. Just in the last decade, new laws have been added to the books to deal with sexual violence, harassment, and other forms of exploitation of women and children.

And, the election of President Clinton in 1992 also ushered in a more hospitable era for women in politics because of his Administration's commitment to making women equal partners and equal voices in government. To that end, he has appointed some of the most talented women ever to serve in government—women like Attorney General Janet Reno, Health and Human Services Secretary Donna Shalala, Energy Secretary Hazel O'Leary, Council of Economic Advisers Chairman Laura D'Andrea Tyson, United Nations Ambassador Madeleine K. Albright, and Environmental Protection Agency Administrator Carol Browner. And as his first Supreme Court nominee he chose Ruth Bader Ginsburg, an accomplished federal judge who overcame enormous gender barriers to rise through the legal profession.

These are indeed proud days for women, and hopefully a sign of more progress to come!

Still, while we should celebrate the triumphs thus far, we must also remember the struggles it took to get here. And we should brace ourselves for the challenges that lie ahead.

One way to continue our progress is to encourage men and women alike to read Barbara Boxer's wonderful book, *Strangers in the Senate,* a personal tale of endurance and success. Boxer, a former stockbroker, journalist, and local county official, challenged the conventional wisdom about women in government by running for Congress, tackling some of the most difficult issues facing the nation, and winning election to the House of Representatives five times and most recently to the U.S. Senate.

Her hard-fought Senate campaign in California in 1992 was more than a symbolic victory for women. The nation's most populous state spoke volumes by choosing two savvy, tough and compassionate politicians—Barbara Boxer and former San Francisco Mayor Dianne Feinstein—as its top representatives on Capitol Hill.

Senator Boxer is more than a role model for young women interested in political careers. She is a pioneer who helped shatter the glass ceiling in Congress and forever transform one of America's traditional male political bastions. She also is a devoted wife and mother whose family's support was crucial to her success in the public realm.

Like so many women in our history who paved the way for others, Senator Boxer epitomizes the highest ideals of public office—to serve the people and the nation. I am especially grateful that a woman of her intelligence, energy and commitment had the courage to fight discrimination and historical odds to land where she is today.

—Hillary Rodham Clinton
August, 1993

PART I

FLASHPOINT

Chapter One

The March

On the way to a campaign speech on Saturday, October 6, 1991 I heard the breaking news report that the nomination of Clarence Thomas to the Supreme Court had hit a possible snag due to allegations by a very distinguished law professor that he had sexually harassed her while she was employed by him.

Although I hate to admit any political misjudgment, especially this early in the book, I feel compelled to say that I made a major goof. I thought it was over for Clarence Thomas. I said out loud, "That's it. Bush will pull the nomination."

Since I was very worried about Thomas's views on a number of issues and Thomas's blatant ducking of the choice issue in front of the Senate Judiciary Committee on September 12, 1991, I looked forward to a new African-American nominee who would at least be more flexible and less ideological on abortion and economic justice issues—or at the very least, a nominee who wouldn't say that he had never discussed *Roe v. Wade* at law school, or with anyone, ever! I breathed a sigh of relief and at my campaign appearance suggested that a new nomination was probably in the making.

Inside the Beltway

It is often said that Washington is two nations—one inside the Washington, D.C. beltway, and the other the rest of the country. So when I returned to Washington Monday night and headed to the House of Representatives, where I served, I was doubly stunned to learn that not only would President Bush stick with his nominee, but that the Senate did not plan to air the charges of sexual harassment fully. Thomas's nomination process, it was said, was a wrap.

It's hard to describe my feelings. Here was a man who had spent eight years (1982-1990) as the head of the Equal Employment Opportunity Commission (EEOC), the very agency charged with enforcing sexual harassment laws! Here was a man who would interpret those laws on the Supreme Court, perhaps for as long as 30 or 40 years. And yet, in spite of the serious nature of the charges, it was to be business as usual. If a different charge, like fixing a basketball game while in college, had emerged, would there have been at least a time out, I wondered.

But there was no time out after Anita Hill came forward. So on Tuesday morning, October 8, 1991, I left my office and went over to the floor of the House of Representatives, and, as if it had been planned, most of the Democratic women of the House did the same.

Sixty Seconds of Fame

Andy Warhol suggests that everyone gets 15 minutes of fame. In the House, fame is doled out in 60-second intervals. Well, there we were, about ten women, and we began speaking during the "one minutes." As every member of the House, as well as every C-SPAN junkie, knows, "one minutes" are the time for Members of Congress to speak out on any issue.

So on this day, after the stunning developments in the Clarence Thomas nomination, the women began to speak out, without any previous planning.

Take Time for Justice

On that fateful day, the female members of the House stood up and spoke their minds. Representative Louise Slaughter of New York started off with an important reminder:

> Mr. Speaker, we vest enormous power in judges in this country. A judge can take away your family, your children, your business, your liberty, and that is why we take great care in choosing people who serve in the judiciary, no less those who serve in the Supreme Court of the United States, a lifetime appointment.
>
> A young woman, a woman with a good background, took the courage and the time to try to say that there were some allegations about the present nominee that should be investigated, and the usual cry goes up from men all over the country, "Too late, too late, should have told us about it earlier. Why did she wait around? It couldn't have been much. We're going along with the dance."
>
> Mr. Speaker, that is the reason why women in this country are so afraid to come forward with allegations of sexual harassment. That is why Congress has written laws making it possible for them to come forward with allegations of sexual harassment. That is why the Congress should make certain that allegations are checked thoroughly.

If this nominee is confirmed he has the possibility of serving 40 years with this allegation hanging over him. For the rest of her life, Professor Hill will be faced with the fact that she came forward to this committee and made these allegations.

Surely, for the sake of both of them, for their reputations and their future, time must be taken to look at these thoroughly and dispose of them properly.

Pat Schroeder of Colorado was next:

Mr. Speaker, this is a nation that has always prided itself in always having time for justice. Think about our symbol of justice, a scale, a scale where the woman is blindfolded and cannot see who says what and everyone's words weigh equally. It does not say that someone is empowered to say, "Well, a Supreme Court nominee's words weigh heavier than someone else's, or someone else's words weigh heavier." No. It is equal.

Nor is there a clock behind that scale of justice saying, "Oh, time ran out. Take the scales away. That's it."

Nor does it say we can defer to an FBI official, or someone else, an elected representative's responsibility to take the time to be fair.

Mr. Speaker, we are at a very critical time in which a woman has come forward and made very serious allegations, and there is an attempt to brush them under the rug in the speed to have an adjournment for the Columbus Day recess. Columbus, I think, would even be appalled that we could be hurrying home to celebrate this great Nation, and also tainting this great Nation's reputation for justice.

Mr. Speaker, I hope justice prevails. I hope we can take time to listen to everyone and weigh their words.

Then, in an attempt to discredit the women members, Representative Dana Rohrabacher from California gave the following "one minute":

Mr. Speaker, the last minute personal attack on Judge Thomas is another example of the gutter level politics which is now the standard operating procedure for liberals in America.

Liberalism has been rejected by the people, with its reliance on high taxes, large bureaucracy, and social nonsense which is contrary to fundamental American values.

So not having the support of the people for their views, liberals now rely on personal attacks—vicious, mean spirited, often untruthful abuse of people who disagree with them. Liberals are making Joe McCarthy look like a nice guy.

Someday the public is going to realize that the personal attacks on anyone who disagrees with liberals are part of a pattern—a pattern that is contrary to our national spirit. Has liberalism really sunk to this nasty, destroy your opponent style of politics?

Liberals. Have you no sense of decency?

Confirm Judge Thomas. Reject gutter politics.

Following his display, I rose to speak:

Mr. Speaker, imagine yourself dependent on another human being for your livelihood. Imagine the power that person holds over you. Imagine that person making suggestive comments to you, and beyond that, telling you in detail about pornographic materials he had seen. Would you be intimidated?

Yes, especially if you are in your twenties and you are a woman in a man's field. Intimidation like that is against the law. Indeed, our law protects women in the workplace from that type of harassment.

And which court is that final protection of women from this kind of harassment? Which court has that awesome responsibility to protect our society from those who would harm its most vulnerable citizens? The Supreme Court of the United States of America.

Where are those in Congress who talk about pornography every other day? Why are they not leading the charge for a delay?

This is not pleasant. This is not happy and it's not pretty. Neither is sexual harassment, whether you were touched or verbally demeaned.

To respect women in this society means you give these charges your attention, and when you are confident about the truth, however long it takes, beyond a reasonable doubt, it will be time to vote.

Gag Rules

Then Congresswoman Rosa de Lauro of Connecticut began her comments and there was a loud interruption from the Republican side of the House. Using an arcane rule, they tried to stop her very legitimate speech.

The arcane House rule Rosa was "breaking" involved using the word "Senate" in her speech; odd as it sounds, in referring to the Senate, as a member of the House, you could say the "other body" or the "upper body" (which House members detest saying) but you couldn't say the word "Senate." The rule has since been changed, but at the time, Rosa was committing a minor transgression.

The Republican men tried to stop her speech on the grounds that it was against the rules of the House to talk about what was going on in the Senate. As far as I was concerned, the whole world was talking about what was going on in the Senate. This rule was ludicrous, and the Republicans' insistence on following it was just as absurd.

Rosa wanted to make another statement, this time technically in order but basically saying the same thing, but the Republicans objected to her speaking again and we had to call a vote of the House to see if she could do so.

Obviously, our Republican friends didn't care about that rule or even Rosa's speech. They simply wanted to stop our talk, break our stride—a common technique used in debate, especially since C-SPAN started televising House proceedings.

But by this time, our remarks were starting to strike a nerve in the country. Women were calling Capitol Hill in unprecedented numbers. The Congresswomen were getting most of the calls because women across the country felt that we "got it" and that we understood their outrage that the nomination was going through as if nothing had happened.

The Republican "procedural" challenge stopped the "one-minutes" while a 15-minute vote was called to see if, under the rules, Congresswoman DeLauro could make her remarks.

Schroeder's Strategy

As the voting began, Congresswoman Pat Schroeder, 20-year House veteran and dean of the women House members, presented me with a two-part strategy. While some of the women members would stay on the House floor to ensure that we won the vote to un-gag Rosa, the rest of us would walk over to the "other house," where our Senate colleagues were meeting on this very subject, to give them our view of what was going on in the country and to let them know that we believed the charges were serious—and in need of further investigation.

I remember clearly that Congresswoman Nancy Pelosi remained on the House floor with Rosa, effectively explaining to our colleagues that it was important that Rosa continue her remarks. Meanwhile, I grabbed Congresswomen Eleanor Holmes-Norton, Louise Slaughter and Jolene Unsold. Pat got Nita Lowey and Patsy Mink, and we all briskly walked out of the House chamber and over to the Senate steps.

As often happens when people act in synch, there was little talking as we walked. We didn't plan what we would tell the Senators but we knew that we'd tell them the truth about what we were feeling. And we knew that we would be of help to them—and we wanted to be of help; with only two women in the Senate, they could use our perspective. We felt that we would be welcome, or that at least our advice would be welcome.

Climbing the Senate Steps

We didn't expect the numbers of cameras facing us. When we moved toward the Senate steps, we saw them... still photographers, TV cameras, tape recorders, hand mikes, boom mikes and flash bulbs.

"Where are you going?"

"To speak to the Senators."

"Why?"

"To tell them the charges are serious."

"What do you want them to do?"

"Slow down and look at the charges."

"Was Thomas guilty?"

"We don't know. We just think the charges are serious."

We left the cameras and climbed the stairs of the Senate and went to the doors, behind which sat our colleagues, discussing the Thomas nomination and how to handle it. This was their usual Tuesday luncheon meeting—the Democratic caucus lunch.

I remember a crush of staff people asking who we were as we approached a set of large mahogany doors. I distinctly remember someone saying we were seven Congresswomen who very much wanted to meet with our colleagues for just a few minutes and that it was important. The answer was "no."

We didn't take no to be an acceptable answer.

We knocked on the door. It opened a crack. "You can't come in," said a senior staffer. Someone, I think it was Congresswoman Slaughter, said, "For goodness' sake, we're members of Congress. Please ask." The staffer came back. "You can't come in." We huddled together in disbelief but decided to go for a compromise.

"Can we meet with the Majority Leader now?"

"No, you can meet with him later, after the caucus is over."

"There won't be any point after the caucus is over!"

I said, "We want to let the Senators know what we think *before* the caucus is over, so that they can consider our thoughts and advice on how to handle this thing."

"No," the answer came back.

It looked hopeless. But then my political antenna went up and I made one more try.

"Listen, there are about 100 cameras out there and they all took our picture going up the Senate steps," I told one female staffer. "They know what we came over about and they'll want to know what happened. If we don't at least meet with the Majority Leader. . . . " My voice trailed off.

"One moment," she said. "Wait there." *She* got it.

"Okay," she said returning to the door. "The Majority Leader will see you in the side room now."

Knocking on the Door

The day we knocked on that door was an extraordinary circumstance, as history has since shown. The seven of us were the only group of women in the country who could get at all close to where the decision over Clarence Thomas would be made.

It's hard for me to explain how it felt for seven grown women, experienced in life and in politics, to have to pound on a closed door, to have to beg to be heard on a crucial issue that couldn't really wait for niceties.

I don't know if we could have handled it better or differently. I only know that since the confirmation train was headed down the track, we simply had to be heard, and we didn't have much time.

Well, we finally were heard and there followed a hearing that many feel was a travesty. But what followed then, I believe, changed American politics in a fundamental way.

Maybe these changes would have come about anyway. Maybe the political revolution of women in America would have been triggered by another event. But people tell me the photograph of the seven women "marching" to the Senate gave them hope and a sense of their own power. Some women even called the photo "the women's Iwo Jima." It shook them up. It touched them. It also made some people mad. Even some of my friends.

"Why did you have to make such a spectacle? Why couldn't you have just called them on the phone? Why didn't you make a formal appointment?" they asked.

But sometimes in life you do things because you are moved to do them. And when I reflect on civil rights marches and the fact that my friend from Georgia, Congressman John Lewis, has a metal plate in his head from a beating he took at one of them, what we did was minor. We only knew that sexual harassment is degrading; it's humiliating; it's belittling; it's dehumanizing; it's frightening; and when it's done by someone with authority over you, it traps you in a black hole of darkness. And most of us or someone we knew well had experienced it. So we took a chance and broke the unwritten rules and did what we had to do.

Very interestingly, after I was elected to the United States Senate, in November of 1992 by the people of California, and was at the Senate orientation in January, 1993, a very soft-spoken woman to whom I had been introduced earlier, came up to me and said, "Senator, do you remember me?"

I told her we had been introduced earlier.

"No," she said. "Do you remember me from 1991?"

I didn't.

Then she said: "I was the one who wouldn't open the Senate door!"

I absolutely could not believe that the circle had closed. When I was a candidate in early 1991 no one thought I had a chance. Most of the politically powerful in California closed the door on me; the political "experts" closed the door on me; the usual wealthy contributors closed the door on me; but now the Senate staffer who *literally* closed the door on me was there opening it up because the people of California made it happen—sending not just one, but two women to the United States Senate and making history for our state.

I asked this very courageous staffer, who absolutely never had to identify herself, what she had thought of our walk over to the Senate. I begged her to be honest. She was.

She explained that she responded to the incident as she never had before.

As a Senate staffer whose job it was to ensure that the Senate agenda went smoothly, she was outraged at our behavior. She thought it was "obnoxious"! She also worried that our behavior could make matters worse because she felt that the Majority leader was trying hard to win the votes to delay the Thomas confirmation vote, and that our aggressive tactics could backfire.

But on the other hand, she understood our agony and shared our feelings about the issue. She said she'd never felt so schizophrenic about anything—so torn.

She did tell the Majority Leader that we would be "trouble" if he didn't meet with us and I think she was right on that. Something was going on that was bigger than we were, something that would trigger feelings of anger that would be turned into electoral victories.

"We Don't Let Strangers In"

After our very cordial and important meeting with Majority Leader Mitchell, Pat Schroeder and I were insistent on learning why we couldn't get into the Senate meeting. We were both told the following by a prominent Senator: "We don't let strangers in." That line is the inspiration for the title of this book, and when it was told to me, it knocked me over.

Imagine seven women members of Congress, with 80 years of political experience between them, being thought of as "strangers" in the United States Senate. If that was true for us, what about everyone else?

Later, we learned that in context the word "stranger" meant simply "non-Senator." It didn't mean stranger in the ordinary sense. I felt better knowing that, but I still believe that the more common meaning of the word really was closer to the truth.

The truth is that women have been strangers in the Senate, as you will see . . . strangers in the highest, most powerful legislative body in the world. But because of a revolution that took place in 1992, or at least that has started in cities and towns and counties across America, the days of women as strangers in the Senate are ending.

In this book I will explain the revolution in a very personal way, assess what its impact will be on the nation's agenda, and lay out a strategy for making sure the positive change of inclusion continues.

Why the Revolution Must *Continue*

I truly believe that it must continue—for the good of the world. In February of 1993 a United Nations report quoted a 41-nation survey. It showed that if we don't change the current rate of progress, it will take 500 years before women hold equal managerial posts with men and 475 years after that to reach equal political and economic status. The report cites the "invisibility of women in public life" as being a cause of this problem.

The inclusion of women in the highest legislative halls of the land is an area where America should take the lead. By example, we can show that the vibrancy of our democracy increases as we increase our diversity. Not because women are better, but because women are equal.

We will bring a different perspective to the table, one that has been sorely missing—a perspective that is needed to make our country's policies relevant to the lives of all our people.

But power isn't given up easily. Doors don't open up easily. The doors to the Senate certainly didn't open up easily, as you will see. It's tough and it's rough and it is especially difficult for women because there are higher standards for women.

But it will happen if the people want it to happen . . . and that means men as well as women. Men have daughters and nieces and mothers and aunts. They are part of the revolution, too.

So the doors of the Senate opened a crack in 1992, bringing six women in the Senate—a 200 percent increase in two years!

This book is about the whys, the hows and the future of the new political revolution of women in America. Although it is difficult to make sense of a revolution while it is happening, I don't think we can afford to let it take its course without comment and encouragement. Too much is at stake.

Chapter Two

Anita Hill: A Lightning Rod for Change

I was already running for the United States Senate when the Anita Hill story broke onto the scene. Pollsters and pundits alike said it would be a passing thing. News reports said that in a very short time no one would remember either Anita Hill or the issue of sexual harassment.

My own pollster told me not to stress this issue too much because her data from California confirmed the national data. Most people, including women, believed Clarence Thomas; they did not believe Anita Hill when she said he had sexually harassed her. Most people, women included, thought that the Senate Judiciary Committee had treated Anita Hill fairly; they believed Clarence Thomas should be confirmed to the United States Supreme Court to replace Thurgood Marshall.

I felt something strange was happening here. But deep inside, I knew that although the pollsters were correct in what they were reporting, they couldn't tell us why the answers were coming back the way they were. Why would women react in such a forceful way *against* Anita Hill after all the years of the women's movement and the fight for equal pay for equal work and the fight for choice and equality?

I believed there was more to the story. Perhaps it was a clear case of denial. If women were to believe that Clarence Thomas did something wrong to Anita Hill while he was her boss, then many women who had never questioned what happened to them in the workplace, at home, or on the street, would have to reevaluate their own lives. If they were to believe Anita Hill it would clearly illuminate the powerlessness of women. What did it say about a woman's role in society if such a well-educated lawyer had endured such humiliation? Better not to believe Anita Hill; better to deny it and put it behind us quickly and move on.

But it was not to be, because the months that followed would see what we in politics call the "gotcha syndrome," meaning that other things would happen to underscore the vulnerability of all women, making it impossible to turn away from the truth. The first time, something can fool you, but the second time—gotcha!

According to the *US News and World Report* polling data, in October 1991 only 24 percent of the women in America believed Anita Hill, while 60 percent believed Clarence Thomas. By 1992, 38 percent believed Anita Hill and 38 percent believed Clarence Thomas. And while 58 percent of the women had believed it was right to confirm Judge Thomas as a Supreme Court Justice in 1991, in 1992 that figure had changed to only 44 percent.

Something very significant happened to Americans and in particular to the women of America in the intervening months. At first we didn't want to deal with an issue that was so ugly and personal, an issue that made many of us question ourselves and our decisions. But as time passed we kept thinking about it (and underneath American society lies a rugged individualism) and although the pundits told us that the Anita Hill affair was not important and would go away, we kept thinking about her, and we faced the issues that were raised in the Anita Hill-Clarence Thomas confrontation. And slowly we changed our collective minds.

Aftershocks

Anita Hill's testimony was like an earthquake. Coming from the San Francisco area, I can tell you that when an earthquake occurs we put it behind us as fast as we can; but even when we do, there are always aftershocks that stop us from forgetting.

There were aftershocks to the Anita Hill case. There was Tailhook, the military sexual assault scandal in which innocent women were brutally harassed and molested by Navy men; there were rape trials involving famous men; there were countless stories of harassment, appearing one after the other, by women emboldened to talk. American women added it all up—the earthquake called Anita Hill plus the aftershocks—and they changed their minds about Anita Hill and Clarence Thomas.

In retrospect, the American public realized that Anita Hill struck an honest chord; Clarence Thomas struck a disturbing chord; and the Senate Judiciary Committee, looking like a relic from another time and place, struck a chord of irrelevancy. And all these chords played together had a dissonant sound. America, and in particular, American women, were uncomfortable with the way the whole issue was handled, were uncomfortable with the way the Senate looked—and the Anita Hill incident became a catalyst for change.

Dr. Susan Blumenthal, chief of Basic Prevention and Behavioral Medicine, Research Branch at NIMH, told us in an interview that the anger that was triggered by the hearings was at first directed at Anita Hill. She had raised the sexual harassment issue and awakened within many women feelings that they didn't want to face, whether they were secretaries, professionals, or homemakers. "Everyone had a story to tell," says Blumenthal, "but most had denied the problem, or coped with it."

But then, she says, women started seeing the issue in a different way . . . they saw it as a "power differential" between men and women. And women began to realize that their silence was an admission of their lack of power.

Women began to realize that Anita Hill's discussion of sexual harassment in the most public of forums was giving them the room to speak the truth about their own lives and in that collective truth lay their own "empowerment." Discussions were opened up around the country; organizations started to respond by putting policies on sexual harassment in place, by training employees and enforcing policies.

Women as Outsiders

Hill led women to political empowerment, as women finally made the ultimate connection between their lack of power and the lack of women in high political office. Change became the political slogan of the 1992 elections, and who would personify change more than the people who *weren't* on the Senate Judiciary Committee, who *weren't* ever around President Bush, and who *weren't* ever around the corridors of political power in a meaningful way? *Women were the ultimate outsiders* and 1992 would be the "Year of the Woman," with the November elections tripling the number of women in the Senate and almost doubling the number of women in the House of Representatives.

Blumenthal has an interesting explanation for the changing feelings about Anita Hill. She compares Anita Hill to the "amneoastic response" in immunology. "When you get infected the first time, you may get a small response," says Blumenthal, "but the second time the anti-bodies really respond." So, first there was Anita Hill, she concludes, who sensitized the people; and then there was the Tailhook scandal in the Navy, and Dr. Frances Conley at Stanford Medical Center, who proved that even highly paid physicians could be targets of sexual harassment. By then people were beginning to wake up to the powerlessness of women in the workplace at a time when work is no longer an option but a necessity for most women.

Psychiatrist Martin Blinder of California, a former office holder and courtroom expert witness, agrees with Blumenthal that women are seen as the ultimate outsiders. He also believes that the Anita Hill hearings became such a "caricature of government as usual" that they accelerated the wave of anti-incumbency that sweeps the country "from time to time."

"Because men are in power," reasons Blinder, "the political revolution of 1992 was [a revolution] against the male way of doing things."

But Blinder says it was more than Anita Hill that got women elected. He says that when things are going wrong, women get called in. For example, he points out, companies use women all the time when there is bad news to tell the public. "Instead of having this three-piece-suit, white male come out and say his company never did anything wrong (even though there is cyanide in the aspirin), they bring a woman out, who is perceived as being without authority, so people will believe that the company wasn't responsible."

Where does Blinder's theory lead us? It looks like the more problems we see, the more likely we are to elect women. If that is so, women should get ready for political office, because the policies of the '80s have left us with problems as far as the eye can see. And isn't it always Mom who has to come in, separate the warring children, and clean up the mess?

But when the seven women of the House of Representatives made that famous march over to the U.S. Senate to ask the Senators to look at Anita Hill's charges, we hadn't heard any of this analysis. We didn't know if we were doing a popular thing or an unpopular thing; we didn't know whether it made any difference whatsoever. We only knew that we were uneasy, so uneasy that we were willing to break the unwritten—but strict—rules of the United States Senate and demand that we be heard. We were unladylike about it and we were not sweet about it. We couldn't be.

When I look now at the Associated Press photograph that was on the front page of many newspapers across the country, and I see the look on my face and the faces of my colleagues as we walked, I see determination and conviction. I do not see happiness. Detractors saw that picture and called us every name in the book. They described us as angry and strident.

It has always fascinated me that women are often seen as "strident," while men are "strong"; we're often "loud," while men are "forceful," "opinionated," while men are "smart." One of my greatest supporters and friends, songwriter Marilyn Bergman, reminded me of a presentation by Barbra Streisand in which she said:

A man is commanding—a woman is demanding. A man is forceful—a woman is pushy. A man is uncompromising—a woman is a ballbreaker. A man is a perfectionist—a woman is a pain in the ass. He's assertive—she's aggressive. He strategizes—she manipulates. He shows leadership—she's controlling. He's committed—she's obsessed. He's persevering—she's relentless. He sticks to his guns—she's stubborn. If a man wants to get it right, he's looked up to and respected. If a woman wants to get it right, she's difficult and impossible.

So to many, we were difficult or impossible—but some of our admirers had called us the Magnificent Seven for making that walk. We thought it was a stretch, but it made us grin.

Buried Memories

Many things gave us those determined looks, but I am convinced that our own experiences in life, many of which were buried for 20 or 30 and even 40 years, added to our determination. Women all over the country had locked up certain memories when it came to sexual harassment, and it was no different for the women of the House of Representatives.

Congresswoman Louise Slaughter of New York had the most troubling story. She said that not until the Anita Hill incident did she have the courage to look once again at her experience. As we walked over to the Senate, Louise Slaughter was as determined as I'd ever seen her. A woman with a wonderful sense of humor, she was not showing it on that day. She was angry at the Senate for not immediately holding up the Thomas nomination after Anita Hill's charges surfaced, and she wanted a chance to tell the Senators what she thought about it. But it wasn't until she watched the hearings, sitting behind Anita Hill in the hearing room, that the memories of her own experience with sexual harassment came rushing back to her. She said the memory of this incident had been completely sublimated.

Louise Slaughter represents upstate New York and was born in Harlan County, Kentucky in 1929. The incident that Anita Hill's charges evoked in Louise occurred when Louise was 16 years old. She told me that as she watched the men of the Senate Judiciary Committee staring down at Anita Hill in the hearing room, she suddenly remembered four of five male doctors surrounding her as she stood stark naked on an examination table with nothing but a flimsy sheet around her. Her mother had driven many miles to Lexington in order to have Louise examined. Something was wrong with her ankle and yet, while her mother was told to wait in the waiting room, the doctors had asked Louise to strip completely. She remembers them asking her to turn around and around as they looked up at her. She said she knew something was very wrong at the time . . . but she was afraid to say anything to her mother or to anyone and of course she didn't dare question any doctor. From that time forward she vowed that she would go to medical school, to spare women that kind of shame. It was not to be. "It wasn't even a possibility in those days," says Louise.

So, Louise Slaughter settled for the next best thing . . . she became a micro-biologist. But she really wanted to become a doctor, so other women wouldn't have to be humiliated in the same way she was. Louise Slaughter's sense of humor does come back as she finishes her story. "They're probably all dead by now," she says of the doctors. "But as I was watching those men on the Judiciary Committee peering down at Anita Hill, I became so filled with emotion. . . . I was so nervous for her. . . . I was like a hen on a hot egg!" She says she wondered then if we had done the right thing for Anita Hill by walking over to the Senate and thereby forcing the hearing.

She knows now it was the right thing for America.

A Personal Story

So many women sublimated these kinds of experiences. When Congresswoman Nancy Pelosi held a fundraiser at her San Francisco home for the New College of Law, in 1991, Anita Hill was the honored guest. Congresswoman Pelosi says that woman after woman came up to Professor Hill to tell her their particular story. These mostly professional women told the woman who gave them the courage to speak out that it was liberating for them to meet her, because she changed their lives for the better, by setting an example. "I had never seen anything like it before," relates Pelosi. "These were all self-assured, successful women bearing their souls to someone they didn't even know, yet someone who had freed them from their secret stories."

When you think that you are the only person in the world to experience such humiliation, it is a very lonely feeling.

I myself had never shared my incident with anyone but my husband. I thought it was unique, but in fact it probably was an everyday occurrence in 1962.

I was an economics major in college and took great pride in my grades—so much so, that when I was caught wearing Bermuda shorts to school underneath my full-length raincoat, I was willing to beg for forgiveness from the dean, rather than have my grades be lowered for the offense.

Well, knowing my history, you can imagine my chagrin when I received a C minus in an economics course in which I believed I was running an A minus. The teacher was known as a very good one and was somewhat the marvel of the campus because he and his wife had a large number of children—I think it was seven—which was highly unusual in those days.

So, this family man gave me a C minus as a final grade and I was very upset. This was my last semester of under-graduate school; I had been married for six months and was thinking of going to graduate school at night while I worked by day to put Stew through law school.

I decided to phone my professor. He suggested that I come up to see him in his office so we could go over the final exam. I asked Stew to drop me off and meet me in 15 minutes outside the main entrance of the campus.

When I walked into the office, my professor asked me to sit down and I asked him right off the bat why he gave me a C minus. I was running such a good average in my major and this was upsetting to me. What followed was this:

"Barbara," he said, "I tell you that I had to bend over backwards to be fair as I graded your paper because you know you are my favorite. You always have such energy and sparkle, and you always engage so actively in the discussion."

"Okay," I said, not having any idea where this was going, "so why did you give me such a rotten grade if I'm so strong in class?"

"Well, it was your final exam," he said.

"I'd like to see it," I said.

"If you want it, I'll send it to you."

By now I was wondering what was with this guy. I came over to see my final exam at his suggestion and now he doesn't even have it.

"But that's why I came here . . . to see my paper," I said.

This discussion was going nowhere, so I got up to leave. (One thing is certain in incidents like this: you remember every detail—just like you remember where you were when JFK was shot—because it's so traumatic.)

When he got up and closed the door, I began to figure out "what was wrong with this picture." But I still hadn't focused on the fact that no one was around because school was out.

"You're graduating, aren't you?" Mr. Family Man asked. "I'm going to miss you. Don't you want to kiss me goodbye?"

"Not really, professor." I walked toward the door and he grabbed me by the shoulders tightly and leaned over to kiss me. Now I remember seeing his "old" face coming at me, my pushing him away, grabbing the door handle and running down the empty corridor to the street in search of Stew's car.

He was there, thank goodness, and I told him the story. He was very angry. He was 23 and I was 21.

We talked about the incident again and again and this is what we concluded: we would not tell anyone. No one would believe me. I was graduating, anyway. Why make trouble, more than likely for myself? We never told anyone . . . not my parents or Stew's mother or our friends or anyone in charge. Now I think it was selfish not to tell, because who knows how many other young women suffered my professor's disgusting advances or his crummy grades? I never got a copy of my exam or an increase in my grade, needless to say.

When I ask Stew about this incident now, his memory jibes with mine. He remembers that I was extremely upset, but that we decided to put it out of our lives. That was 30 years ago—and we both remember an incident that really didn't harm me physically or mentally, except to make me feel temporarily powerless. It dampened my spirit and my dignity.

When people ask why Anita Hill waited so long to talk I feel they misunderstand the insidious nature of sexual harassment; it's usually one person's word against another, and the victim is often made to feel guilty. I'm sure if I had complained to the dean he would have said, "What else can you expect from someone who would dare to wear Bermuda shorts to school?" Today, thanks partially to Anita Hill and the aftershocks, universities are searching for policies to prevent such abuses of power. Sexual harassment is about the abuse of power.

Schroeder on Sexual Harassment

While I was fending off my professor, Congresswoman Pat Schroeder was getting her law degree. In 1964 she worked for the National Labor Relations Board. There she heard story after story—sometimes a union member complaining about advances made by another union member; sometimes it was the boss making advances. But as she listened to these stories of harassment she had to look the complaining woman in the eye and tell her the truth . . . there was nothing in the law to protect her from sexual harassment.

As Pat Schroeder led the walk over to the Senate she remembered those stories. As she fought, as a Congresswoman, for the enactment of monetary damages for sexual harassment and gender discrimination in the workplace, she remembered those stories. (We finally have those punitive damages, though they are limited, unlike those damages for racial discrimination. We need to change that.) Congresswoman Schroeder herself has been on the receiving end of a lot of abuse because of her leadership on the issue of sexual discrimination in the military.

From her senior position on the House Armed Services Committee, she led the Congressional investigation of the Navy's Tailhook scandal. Accepting no white wash, she demanded that the incident be fully examined and the punishment handed down to those responsible.

Pat Schroeder tells me that life has been different since she took on the Navy's culture.

Initially covered up, the Tailhook scandal began when more than 25 women—13 of them Naval officers—were fondled, groped, disrobed, and sexually assaulted by drunken Marine and Navy aviators at the annual convention of the Tailhook Association in September of 1991.

The Tailhook Association is made up of present and former Navy pilots and is named for the hook on the back of Navy planes, enabling them to land on aircraft carriers. After the Tailhook Scandal came to light, the Navy ceased all official relations with the group.

Investigators found that the women were pushed through a line of drunken aviators in a hotel hallway; the incident went on for several hours. In addition to the "gauntlet" of men attacking women, one squadron hosted a suite at the Convention that featured nude strippers, sexual intercourse by a couple in the presence of aviators and "public sex acts" by aviators, according to the investigation report.

Schroeder was not going to back away as initial Navy reports tried to play the incident down. She pushed for an independent investigation originating outside the Navy after an investigative officer reported that the Secretary of the Navy "came by" the suite where lewd activities were taking place. The Secretary had stated that he hadn't learned of the lewd activities until weeks after the convention.

At that point Schroeder was adamant. Although then-Representative Beverley Byron (D-Md.), a colleague of Schroeder's on the Armed Services Committee, was reported in *USA Today* on June 19, 1992 as saying Garrett "is trying to get to the bottom of the issue," Schroeder noted in the same story, "They [the Navy] don't seem able to bring themselves to really clean it up." Then Schroeder linked the Tailhook incident to the unequal treatment women are given in the military, arguing that the glass ceiling keeps qualified female pilots from flying, and thus from being treated with respect.

The boys in the Navy didn't like it. So on June 18, 1992 at the Tomcat Follies, another annual Navy event, they used a skit to attack Schroeder for her toughness on Tailhook in a skit. In the banner featuring the verse, "Hickory, dickory, dock . . . " Schroeder was "invited to perform oral sex," according to a July 3, 1992, *Washington Post* article.

She was lambasted in yet another skit, and then on July 25 she was "treated" to an obscene fax by a Marine stationed in North Carolina, in which "obscene comments were directed at Schroeder and women Marines in general," according to Lt. Colonel Jim Vance, who spoke to the Associated Press on July 25, 1992. The Associated Press reported that the fax consisted of anatomical references to women, "some pictures and a few brief sentences." The Marine who participated in the incident broke at least one military rule of justice, including statutes against the sending of obscene materials across state lines. When this book went to press, no one had yet been punished.

In all of these cases, 20-year Congresswoman Pat Schroeder graciously accepted all apologies rendered, but she never backed down. After each indignity she said publicly that she would continue to press for equality for women in the military as well as for rigorous enforcement of sexual harassment laws.

After the incident at the Tomcat Follies, Schroeder told the States News Service on July 2, 1992 that the banner represented more than a joke to the men during a party—it reflected the attempts of men in the Navy to make women feel "as unacceptable as possible."

In the February 21, 1993 edition of the *Los Angeles Times*, Schroeder was reported as "offering an olive branch" to Navy aviators. But she still refused to back down. While praising the "positive effect" of the independent investigation into Tailhook for which she had worked, she noted that critics have contended that "the Navy routinely ignored incidents of sexual misconduct by fighter pilots." She added that the core values of "courage, integrity and teamwork, encouraged in every member of the Armed Forces," had to be lived up to. And although she praised the Navy for "finally beginning to come around," she also said, "we need to make sure they [the Navy pilots] are living up to those values. That's why we were so aggressive in this area, specifically, Tailhook."

Schroeder was flooded with criticism from unnamed Navy men who said that she had ruined dozens of careers by pressing for an aggressive investigation of Tailhook, and she was further blamed for pressuring officials into disciplining those involved in the Tomcat Follies. Still, Schroeder did not back down. "I don't do discipline," she said. Discipline comes down "through Navy procedures."

But then she got to the heart of the matter, pressuring Congress to give women the go-ahead to fly in combat. "We're not talking about lowering standards," she said. "If women can qualify . . . it would be silly to deny ourselves half the brain power of this country just because they have the wrong chromosomes." (Vintage Schroeder. Twenty years ago, she said she had a brain and a uterus, now she's talking about chromosomes.)

So Pat Schroeder led the march to the Senate in October 1991 to make the point that women could no longer be silent in the face of sexual harassment and discrimination.

The majority of members of the Senate Judiciary Committee made Clarence Thomas a victim either by design or incompetence and made Anita Hill the villain. Less than a year later some Navy men would try to make their colleagues who sexually attacked women the victims and make Pat Schroeder the villain. The fact that they committed atrocious acts of violence isn't the reason their careers were ruined. No, they blame a woman, Pat Schroeder, and they blame the female Naval officers who blew the whistle on both Tailhook and the Tomcat Follies.

One evening Schroeder was dining with her husband, Jim, in an Annapolis restaurant. Several men at the bar recognized her. One came over and identified himself as a fighter pilot.

"You're trying to make me into a Mr. Peepers," he told her angrily.

"Sir," she patiently said, "Tailhook isn't about Mr. Peepers; it's about criminal assaults."

"Look, you haven't proven rape, so what are you talking about?" he shouted at her. The bartender had to ask the men to leave her alone.

Out on the street a woman officer came up and thanked Schroeder. "The officers should have stopped Tailhook," she whispered almost tearfully.

"It's always like that," Pat Schroeder says. "The women need us."

Norton and the EEOC Guidelines

As she marched over to the Senate, Eleanor Holmes Norton, Congresswoman from Washington D.C., knew how much women needed us.

She had been the Chair of the Equal Opportunities Commission prior to Clarence Thomas and she had written the sexual harassment law, which included guidelines of what constitutes sexual harassment.

Congresswoman Norton remembers hearing about the charges on television. A trained lawyer, she watched Anita Hill closely. "I watched her demeanor and knew after five minutes that Anita Hill was credible—very credible. I said to myself, This woman is telling the truth!"

Norton explains that when she arrived on the House floor to talk about the need for a hearing on the charges, she realized that it would take a concerted effort to get the hearing. "They [the Republican Congressmen] kept trying to keep us from talking," she recalls, as if it were yesterday, "and then I realized that we would have to walk over there [to the Senate] or there would never be a hearing and the hearing had to take place.

"If nothing happened and the whole thing went away, the guidelines weren't worth the paper they were written on. The guidelines simply could not fall away given a larger-than-life public controversy," she says, her eyes flashing.

Norton is one of the smartest members of Congress I know. As she is an expert on the Constitution, I always value her judgment. Like so many of the women in politics that I admire, she can take complex issues and explain them clearly and dynamically.

The guidelines that she had written for the EEOC—the guidelines that Clarence Thomas was supposed to enforce to the letter, read as follows:

> Unwelcome sexual advances, requests for sexual favors, and other verbal or physical conduct of a sexual nature constitute sexual harassment when:

1. submission to such conduct is made either explicitly or implicity a term or condition of an individual's employment;

2. submission to or rejection of such conduct by an individual is used as the basis for employment decisions affecting such individual; or

3. such conduct has the purpose or effect of unreasonably interfering with an individual's work performance or creating an intimidating, hostile, or offensive working environment.

Congresswoman Norton knew those guidelines and they were clear.

When she marched to the Senate, she says, "I walked for the guidelines, I walked for the EEOC, I walked for the Supreme Court, I walked for women, I walked for Anita Hill."

But Eleanor Holmes Norton says that most of all she walked for black women. "Black women," she says, "who have had their sexuality trivialized and scandalized; black women who have had their sexuality demeaned just as Clarence Thomas had done to Anita Hill."

Norton explains that "because Thomas was a black man, it was important to wipe away any notion that this was about white women against a black man." She continues, her eyes looking upward as she remembered what happened almost two years ago, "I felt a special obligation to walk.

"As a black woman I identified with Anita Hill, as the former chair of the EEOC and because I wrote the guidelines, I had a special obligation and I believe if we didn't walk the hearing would not have been held.

"This man [Clarence Thomas] had taken the agency [EEOC] down to its knees; he had stopped enforcing the law; he didn't even follow each Supreme Court decision. It was a heartbreak for me to see what he had done.

"The guidelines meant so much to me," she explained, because she knew women would be encouraged to come forward if they knew what sexual harassment was—if it was spelled out. She was, she says, "terribly disappointed that during the hearings, the Senators never had the guidelines explained to them."

As I think back to the march, I remember how proud I felt that Eleanor Holmes-Norton was there with us. I thought for sure that she would be welcomed inside the caucus by the Senators. Here was a woman who could lead them through this mess. But it was not to be—the closest she got was the front of the Senate door, just like the rest of us.

Women on Fire

Those who speak out against the status quo pay a price; but Pat Schroeder knows, as Louise Slaughter knows, as Nancy Pelosi knows, as Eleanor Holmes Norton knows, and as every woman in public life knows, that for too long women didn't dare speak out about their experiences and their views. But what we now know is that our experiences are relevant to America—because women are half of America. And men have a stake in it too because their mothers and daughters and nieces are involved.

Even after all of the publicity from our "march" the pundits disputed the impact Anita Hill would have on the 1992 election. In the *Los Angeles Times Magazine* dated February 2, 1992 (four months after the "march"), author Nina Eason does a great job of capturing the mood in early 1992, quoting candidates Feinstein, Mosely-Braun and myself as we talked about the very positive feeling on the campaign trail toward our U.S. Senate candidacies, and portraying the upbeat mood at women's organizations, which had reaped more dollars than they had ever dreamed of for women candidates—due to Anita Hill.

Yet Eason feels compelled to add in a special boxed analysis in the middle of the piece: "History suggests that women candidates, particularly those perceived as focusing on feminist issues, face an uphill battle." To her credit she adds, "Renewed activism by women could change that."

The campaigns of women who ran for the Senate were set afire by Anita Hill. Women started writing checks to women candidates, which they had never done before in any major way; women started writing checks to the Woman's Campaign Fund, to EMILY's List, to the National Women's Political Caucus and to the National Organization for Women in numbers unheard of previously.

Women ended their years of silence and became the leaders for change in America—and many men joined in.

The Reverend Jesse Jackson said that Anita Hill did for women what Rosa Parks, who refused to go to the back of the bus on December 1, 1955, did for African-Americans.

Each of these women, in their dignified and courageous way, made people feel their own power, their own courage, and their own strength. Then, in 1992, the people turned their personal strength into strength at the polls, electing Bill Clinton President (he got 54 percent of the women's vote) and many women from all parts of the country to the House and the Senate.

Anita Hill, the lightning rod for change, showed the American people what the Senate looked like. On the campaign trail, I would often tell people about the numbers of women in the Senate—in 1991, there were 98 men and two women; there were only 28 women out of 435 in the House. But in a world filled with statistics, their eyes glazed over. But for three days, in hour after hour of hearings, America saw the Senate through the Judiciary Committee. Finally they understood what we said many times during the campaign—that "ninety-eight to two just won't do." Eventually they agreed with Dianne Feinstein, who often said in her campaign, "two percent may be good for milk, but it's not good enough for the United States Senate." These slogans had meaning only because Americans had seen for themselves. And they realized that if the Senate is to govern with a sense of relevancy and fairness, we must be a relevant, diverse institution. It's only fair.

PART II

PRELUDE

Chapter Three

A Political Odyssey

From the 1950s to the 1970s—A Personal Revolution, But Small Steps For Womankind

In 1972, I made my first run for local political office. That was the same year that Patricia Schroeder first ran for Congress. She won. I lost.

Ten years later, we were to meet in the House of Representatives—she as a 10-year Congressional veteran from Colorado and the dean of the women members of Congress, and I as a freshman Congresswoman from California. In the ten years since, Congresswoman Schroeder and I have often compared notes about what it was like to run for public office as a woman in 1972.

"Brains As Well as A Uterus"

Pat, a graduate of Harvard Law School, had a bright legal mind and solid experience. The war in Vietnam was raging, and the country was torn apart, with every Congressional race in America riveted on the subject. Despite this issue of life and death, candidate Schroeder spent an inordinate amount of time answering questions about her young children. Pat's declaring that she had "a brain as well as a uterus" didn't stop the questions.

"But what do you do with your children? After all, you and your husband work!" These questions kept coming at Rotary Club after Rotary Club, Chamber of Commerce after Chamber of Commerce.

Finally, Pat Schroeder used the incomparable sense of humor which was to serve her very well in the House. "Well," she said, "Jim and I get up very early—about 6 a.m. We bathe and dress the children and feed them a wonderful breakfast. Then we put them in the freezer, leave for work and when we come home, we defrost them. And we all have a lovely dinner together. They're great!"

Now maybe if I had handled my 1972 campaign with such flair, I would have been elected to the Marin County Board of Supervisors. But it wasn't to be.

I remember when my husband Stew and I welcomed one of my opponents to our home on a sunny weekend in 1971. He wanted to have a "private talk."

What followed was hardly a talk, but rather a condescending attempt to push me out of the race, which had three candidates in it—the incumbent, the aforementioned, and me.

I had decided to make the race because no one else from the progressive environmental community could, or would. How did I get myself into it? Running for office was nowhere on my personal radar screen, not even a tiny part of my carefully scripted life.

Traditional Expectations, Non-traditional Results

I was a child of the '50s—the time of "Happy Days" and Doris Day movies—the Debbie Reynolds days when pert women with personalities that glowed danced their way through what was the "perfect" life and right into the arms of Eddie Fisher guys who would sing to them 'til their dying days—the days when any woman who dared to dream of being a United States Senator would have immediately been referred for mental tests. Even women who merely voted differently than their husbands were said to be exhibiting neurotic tendencies.

Politics? It wasn't even in the realm of the possible for women. As we sagely note today there was "an absolute absence of role models." True, there was Margaret Chase Smith, Senator from Maine, whom my mother pointed to with pride even though the Senator was a Republican and my mother an FDR Democrat to the core. "Imagine what she must be like," my mother used to say. "One woman among all those men. She must be something!" But Margaret Chase Smith was a rarity in the world in which I grew up—an oddity, a blip, not a prelude of things to come.

No, I did what was expected of a middle-class, first-generation American—and fortunately for me, it suited me fine. Born in New York, I got a wonderful education in the public school system—kindergarten through Brooklyn College. I fell in love before the age of 20 and got married at 21 while still a senior in college. I worked to send my husband through law school and by age 27 we had two beautiful (I'm not objective) children.

But now that I look back, there were clues that I might someday break the mold.

In high school, my best friend Juliette and I became the first "girl" coaches of the "boys-only" baseball team. There were no girls sports back in the '50s, so we did the next best thing. It doesn't sound too revolutionary now, but in those days it caused a enough of a stir to rate a news story in the *Brooklyn Eagle*, which became the first "Barbara" clipping in my mother's memory drawer. (When she died, I found it fading on that very old Xerox paper that was shiny and smelly.) I was named "all around camper" at summer camp more than once and was also voted "Miss Wingate" by my high school—a competition which was not a beauty contest but to recognize a kind of "all purpose leader."

At Brooklyn College, which I entered in 1958, I chose economics as my major and political science as my minor, while 90 percent of "the girls" majored in education as a sure-fire way to a good job. In those days, there were very few jobs for women with as many benefits as teaching.

Lest you think I was too much of a trailblazer, you should know that my few unusual thrusts into the male domain were somewhat offset by my enthusiastic service as a cheerleader for Brooklyn College's winless but spirited basketball team. The cheerleaders were co-ed, though. I remember my young husband delicately asking me to give up cheerleading "now that you are a married woman." I didn't want to, but I did.

(I always say that cheerleading was good practice for serving in Congress—especially in the pre-Clinton years, when we lost on so many issues to the George Bush veto. Serving as a Democratic Congresswoman with George Bush, the King of the Veto—he successfully vetoed 44 bills—was like winning the basketball game only to have the win reversed after the videotape replay. We would work hard for the majority vote and pass the bill, but only once did we get two-thirds of the majority necessary to override a veto.)

My first fight against "injustice" occurred when I was 21 and married. Stew and I had moved into a new one-room efficiency apartment on a pretty street called Ocean Parkway. We faced the back, which was cheaper; I think the rent was $90 a month in 1962. The landlord had promised to finish the lobby, which was unpainted and uncarpeted. It had a fancy fountain in the center but that couldn't compensate for the mess that you made when you tracked cement dust into your apartment. After a couple of months went by with no action from the landlord I decided enough was enough. I typed up a petition and took it up to every apartment in the building and presented it to the landlord. We got the carpet. I always get things done when I feel a sense of outrage. I'm sure if I wind up in a nursing home, I'll be organizing for better custard.

A Woman's Place

When I graduated from college as a married woman in 1962, my economics degree in hand, I began my search for a job on Wall Street. With my husband in Fordham Law School, I was the one to earn the tuition; Brooklyn College had been free, but Fordham was costly for us. (Public education is a very emotional issue for me because a quality public education was what I got. Of course, my political detractors point to me as living proof that public education is a failure, but I'll put my public education up against any private school education any day. The situation is different now and we need to fix it.)

But public school education or private school education, a woman could not get a job as a stockbroker on Wall Street in 1962—period! I didn't know that as I started knocking on doors trying to get into a training program, but I found it out pretty fast. (When I met Justice Ruth Bader Ginsburg, we shared stories of the prejudice against women seeking jobs in law or securities in those years. We agreed that it was a very tough time.) I watched longingly as my male counterparts landed spots in all the good firms, but at firm after firm I was told that "women aren't stockbrokers."

I settled for a secretarial position while I studied for the stockbroker's exam on my own. (Fortunately, my mother had told me to learn typing and stenography—"In case there was another Depression or you wind up without a husband, those skills could help you out.") I went to work at an old-line firm for a woman who was an expert in municipal bonds. Each week she put out a broadly read newsletter for "the street" on the municipal bond market; I helped her put it together. After a long while, I got the courage up to ask her why she never signed the newsletters with her first name, which was Elizabeth. She just wrote "E." and her last name, which was Cook. She explained to me that if the men on the street knew that the newsletter was written by a woman, they would never read it!

This kind of discrimination—the kind I faced as a novice on Wall Street and the kind Elizabeth Cook faced as the definitive expert on municipal bonds—was simply accepted as normal. I didn't complain about it, nor did she. In retrospect, our silence is as shocking as the prejudice, but that's the way it was then. As Kate Millet wrote in *Sexual Politics* in 1969, "Many women do not recognize themselves as discriminated against; no better proof could be found of the totality of their conditioning." Sexual prejudice was wrong, but so was racial discrimination, and it took several more years of watching the civil rights movement in action to wake up the women of America to the fact that they were being discriminated against, too.

When I passed the stockbroker exam in the early '60s—without having had the benefit of a training program—I was very excited to tell my bosses, so that I could begin buying and selling securities for the clients I knew I could serve. But when I told them the great news, my bosses were not impressed; they told me I could not earn commission there. So I left and found a firm that figured out that my commission meant dollars for them. That's the thing about equality—it helps everybody.

You Either Withdraw Or You Reach Out

In 1963 I was working to build my commissions when the news came over the Associated Press wire that President John F. Kennedy had been assassinated.

It was a horrific blow.

Not that I was political then. We were too busy working hard for our goals: Stew's law degree, enough savings for a down payment on a home and to start a family.

We were doing what was normally done in those days. We were working toward the American dream. We were the generation that could easily do better then the one before—if we played by the rules. And the rules were education. Education, more education and hard work.

My parents never owned a home; Stew's family never owned a car. My mother never graduated from high school. Before he died, when Stew was 11, Stew's father earned about $35 per week as a truck driver; his mother was a school crossing guard.

President Kennedy stood for our hopes and our dreams. (Bill Clinton has that quality and has obviously been inspired by the Kennedy legacy.) When people say that Kennedy never did much as a President I always respond that although he didn't have much time, his impact on the American people, every single day, was enormous. He made us feel that we could do anything as a people, and that we were a good people. I think of JFK's assassination as the beginning of the end of the old Barbara Boxer; the tragic deaths of Martin Luther King, Jr. and Robert Kennedy completed the change. I would never be the same.

In 1965, after the assassination of John F. Kennedy and before the assassinations of Martin Luther King, Jr. and Bobby Kennedy, Stewart and I moved to California.

Why? Because we thought it was beautiful. We had visited relatives in the San Francisco Bay Area and fallen in love with what we saw—a livable city with a slower pace and charming architecture that reminded us of Europe. There was the possibility of affording a home in a lovely neighborhood—and the sense that had we stayed in New York we would have felt pressure to earn lots of money, because even then it was terribly expensive to live there.

When I arrived in California, Stew was finishing up his finals at law school. I thought I had two months before our first baby to find us a place to live. Wrong! Doug decided he was so excited to see San Francisco that he was born the very next day—two months early. It was scary. When we knew the baby was on the way, we tried to get Fordham Law School to let Stew miss one final so that he could be there for the birth. But they said that if he left, he wouldn't graduate. (So much for family values.)

Stew will never forget how he learned that Doug was born—a note went all through the exam room announcing his fatherhood. He didn't know, then, that Doug was given only a 50 percent chance to live. But the baby was very strong, and he made it.

We settled in San Francisco, and in 1967 Nicole was born—also early. We were better prepared, though she was a little less premature than Doug had been and never in danger. Before we moved from San Francisco to Marin County, where the homes were more affordable, I took the children on their first peace march. I don't remember exactly where it started; I do remember that it wound up in Golden Gate Park. Although we were very much involved in raising our small children and figuring out our future, Stew and I were opposed to the war. We knew we had to do something to help end the war.

In 1968 we moved to the suburbs and in June, while Stew was driving the babysitter home, I watched Robert Kennedy's assassination, live, on TV. I was stunned beyond belief—and I was frightened. I was 28 years old, with two small children, and my country was so violent that it felt out of control—John Kennedy, Martin Luther King, Jr., and now, Bobby Kennedy.

How could I sit back and do nothing to change the violent America of the '60s? Having grown up in the sheltered America of the '50s, I could only imagine how our children would view their world when their leaders were torn away, one by one. It felt like it would never stop. Looking back on it, I had two choices: I could either psychologically withdraw into a 1950s-type bomb shelter and put the family into it, protected from the pain, or reach out and try to change things.

I reached and I guess I haven't stopped reaching since.

Transformation

This wasn't an easy transformation and it certainly had to be difficult for my husband. He must have felt like he married Debbie Reynolds and woke up with Eleanor Roosevelt! Almost overnight our American dream home in Marin County, which we bought for $40,000 in 1967 with a $156 monthly mortgage payment, became like Grand Central Station. The kids still remember endless stacks of envelopes being addressed and stuffed on the kitchen table, spilling over to the dining room, as they played around the edges.

We organized to help low-income, teenage drop-outs get jobs; we organized to save the beauty of our county; we organized to end the war in Vietnam. And the "we" were women like me—college-educated young moms who were thrust out of their traditional lives by events beyond their control. Perhaps this was one stage of the political revolution of the women in America, but it had nothing to do with making life better for women. It was about saving our country for our families and the families of the future. There were campaigns for local ballot initiatives and progressive candidates like George Brown for U.S. Senate (I'm proud to say that Congressman Brown from Southern California was one of my biggest supporters when I ran for the United States Senate 20 years later).

Despite the excitement, things weren't going well. The war ground on and on and came into our own living room, shattering whatever suburban calm was left.

In 1970, Marin County voters placed a peace initiative on the ballot. Everyone said we'd lose, since we were a Republican county and Republicans tended to support Richard Nixon and the war.

Everyone working on the project was a volunteer. I did publicity for the campaign. Surprising even ourselves, we won the vote and a message was sent to President Nixon from Republican Marin County: End the war!

For me, those were non-stop days: the Education Corps; Marin Community Video; the founding of the Kentfield After School Child Care Center, which still exists; Woman's Way (an early women's support group), the Marin Alternative, a progressive, grassroots local political organization. I was a catalyst and had no problem passing off the reins of the projects I helped to begin. If a project is worthy it will transcend the personalities of its founders.

All of this activism led to that weekend in 1971 and my first political candidacy. Lest you think I was the unanimous choice, I must let the record show that the logical choice was Stewart. He was an attorney with a fine future—and he was a man! That meant he was electable. But Stew backed out. We simply couldn't afford to pay the mortgage, take care of the family and put enough away for the kids' education on the $11,000 a year County

Supervisor's salary. So there it stood: I was to be the first serious female candidate in the county in 20 years.

There had only been one female supervisor in Marin since 1850, when Marin became an official county—Vera Schultz, and she ran in the '50s.

Vera Schultz was extraordinary. Because of her, the Marin Civic Center was built by Frank Lloyd Wright. It was Wright's last completed public building and has been a major source of pride and revenue for the community.

I almost made it in 1972, which startled the pundits. But the challenger who visited our home in 1971 and tried to push me out of the race was convinced that I had no business in the race—not because of my views or personality or skills, but because I was a woman.

As he settled down in our living room, he told Stewart and me that he had a great idea. His great idea was that I should drop out of the race. And to talk me into it, he carefully explained that I should drop out, not only because I was a very weak candidate, but because my candidacy and possible victory would be harmful for women. This was quite a twist. How could anyone make the case that a woman who was for woman's issues would hurt women should she win? This is how it was explained to me in 1971: "Only the oppressor can free the oppressed."

If Barbara Boxer was elected to the County Board of Supervisors I would hurt the cause of women's equality because I was oppressed and my actions would be perceived as being in my own self-interest, rather than in the best interest of women. This man actually sat in my living room and said that! But unlike my rejections on Wall Street ten years earlier, this was too much. Giving full credit to the early voices of the women's movement, who told us not to take that garbage, I basically escorted him to the door, suggesting along the way that he drop out! He came in last in a three-way primary race, and I came in first. In the run-off he endorsed the incumbent male and I lost by a hair. I guess that was his way of freeing the oppressed.

Chapter Four

A Political Odyssey

From 1972 to 1992—A Minus to a Plus

I can unequivocally say from direct experience that being a woman running for office in 1972 was a distinct, quantifiable disadvantage. All you had to do was ask people— you found out pretty quickly.

A woman running in those years constantly had her inner strength tested. In her book *Women in Power,* psychologist Toni Bernay says that to be a successful politician, a woman has to listen to "inner applause"—that is, the approval that she continually received as a child when she reached out for new achievements.

In 1972, to be a woman in politics was almost a masochistic experience, a series of setbacks without a lot of rewards. If I was strong in my expression of the issues, I was strident; if I expressed any emotion as I spoke about the environment or the problems of the mentally ill, I was soft; if I spoke about economics I had to be perfect, and then I ran the risk of being "too much like a man." Then there were the Catch-22s. If you were married, why would you do such an unconventional thing as run for office?

STRANGERS IN THE SENATE

And if you were single, what was wrong with you? If you were divorced—forget it!

What kept me going were the issues—always the issues. Like Barbra Streisand's character said in the movie "The Way We Were," "I'm an issues person." And I suppose what also kept me going was the inner applause. I certainly didn't get much outer applause.

Taking the Hits

Any woman who survived a run for public office in those years learned how to take the hits over and over again, and if she was lucky, she learned not to take it personally. On some level she had to know that this was the stuff of pioneers, although it certainly wasn't considered in that way back then. Now, with 20 years experience, I *know* it was the stuff of pioneers.

In 1992, it was different. Being a woman running for public office in 1992 was a distinct advantage. The polls showed it. "Put a woman against a man in the California Senate race in 1992 and all else being equal, she wins," said my pollster, Mark Melman. It wasn't quite as easy as that in 1992, because all else is never equal; in fact, it was the hardest thing I ever did. But as my friend and former boss John Burton says, "Nothing good comes easy," and in 1992 being a woman was absolutely a help.

What happened to change the public's attitude towards women running for office in 1992 from 1972? Clearly, there was a desire for change, but it was more. It was the women's political movement: the painful, wrenching, slow political education of the men and women of America that began anew in the '60s. Finally, voters began to understand that in a country with as many challenges as we face, we need to draw from the largest possible pool of talent to fill positions at the highest levels of legislative power. Particularly in politics, it is essential that every perspective be represented around the table or we will come up with solutions that will fall far short of the task. Worse, we may never get the relevant problems on the national agenda.

The early voices of the modern women's movement— Gloria Steinem, Betty Freidan, to name just two—deserve a great deal of credit. Their words gave so many women the courage to give voice to their own thoughts and feelings. They built on the progress toward equality in the workplace that was made in the '40s, the progress that came about only because of the emergency of a world war.

But what made the job of the feminists so hard in the '60s was that the voices of the '40s had been stilled in the '50s, as our society worried that women like Rosie the Riveter, who went toe to toe with any man on the assembly line, would refuse to step back and let the men regain their superior place in the American workforce.

In the '50s it became almost unpatriotic to hold down a decent-paying job if you were a woman. First, you were made to feel that you were taking that job away from a man, unless you were a secretary or a "helper"—and even a "helper" had to be sure she knew her "place." When I was a teenager, I clearly remember my mother feeling extremely sorry for those women who "had" to work. But mixed in with her sympathy was a definite tone of disapproval. (In later years, however, my loving mother was my strongest supporter.)

As I look back now on the campaign I waged for the Board of Supervisors in Marin County in 1972, I realize what I was up against. To those women and men who had lived through the '50s, I seemed a complete rebel; I was not to be trusted; I was not the kind of woman I should have been. And unfortunately for me, in 1972, the entire electorate had lived through the '50s! In 1992, the voting population had an entirely different profile, with many of those voting born in the '60s and '70s.

But as I study the decade of the '50s, and its black-and-white view of a woman's place, I marvel at the fact that I ever had the nerve to run for public office at all. And as I look back at those times, I understand why I lost that race in 1972.

My own mother-in-law was at a loss to understand why I had run for the Board of Supervisors in 1972. She was slightly embarrassed that I wanted to work at all. She asked some very troubling questions for her, including, "Isn't Stew making an excellent living as an attorney?" I explained that I found it impossible to let our country drift into a war abroad and ignore priorities at home while I sat on the sidelines hoping things would get better for her grandchildren. My mother-in-law nodded and I know she loved me. But I also know she never understood me.

The '50s Model of Women

In 1947, when I was seven years old, wartime slacks were replaced with an ultra-feminine dress design that featured a tight waist and a flared skirt. Christian Dior, the designer who introduced the "New Look," advised women to wear small tight corsets to take a couple inches off their waists.

In the '50s, when I was about 14, I remember wearing cinch belts and layers of crinolines as well as hoop skirts. This was not the outfit of an uppity woman—try anything in crinolines and hoops and you'll understand. Little did I know then that these fashion items were part of American society's move away from the push toward equality for women that had taken place during World War II, when working women had become an important part of building America's war machine to defeat the Nazis.

Writer Michelle Gatlin, in her book *American Women Since 1945*, calls the fashions part of the "post-war feminine mystique," and "part of an ideology which masked women's subordination by calling it female nature or duty."

She says that feminism was "demoted to the status of a simple-minded, outmoded and dangerous ideology."

I can say that I never heard of the word "feminist" in the '50s; I can also say that the post-war feminine mystique intensified women's distrust of one another. Like everyone else, I believed that girls could not be fully trusted as friends because they would always be in competition with you for a boyfriend. I had one very best female friend and I was wary of the others.

Given that history, it is very fortunate that I was able to change completely when I realized, by only half listening to the voices of the women's movement of the '60s, how wrong I had been. I left that part of the '50s behind me.

As I read the sociological history of those days, I also realize how hard my political transformation must have been for my husband. I appreciate how much he has grown despite all the societal "norms" he grew up with, which were reinforced by the popular new medium of the '50s, television.

TV was a powerful way to "show" what life was supposed to be like. In the late '50s came the "soaps," mimicking the shows I used to listen to on the radio. Women in all kinds of emotional situations, always carrying out their proper roles, or getting in trouble if they didn't; commercials that showed women how to clean their homes to a spit-shine in order to be loved and cherished.

Sit-coms showed women with a little more pizzazz— but never in the workplace. "I Love Lucy" featured the incomparable Lucille Ball as a wife who wants to get into show biz. Involved in hilarious pranks each week, she always messed up, proving to her husband that she had better just stay home. In the '50s, no television show that I can remember ever portrayed women in the workplace— let alone in the United States Senate!

Rosie the Riveter was gone, though her life hadn't been that rosy, as was pointed out in a documentary in 1988. "She and her war plant co-workers were paid less then men," wrote Leo Schigsohn for *Newsday*, as he reviewed the show. "Black women were paid less than white women and attempts to equalize were considered un-patriotic. But despite this, the war effort gave the women the chance to make more money than they had ever made before." There were clearly fears that women would try to hold on to their jobs as the men came home.

As in Penny Marshall's 1992 movie "A League of Their Own," these women were forced to hang up their cleats and go home—either to the kitchen or to the lower paid domestic or unskilled work they did before the war.

After the war psychiatrists talked about the horrible lives awaiting women who stayed in the workplace.

In her book *The Woman's Movement*, psychoanalyst Helene Deutsch called women "passive, masochistic and narcissistic." In *The Psychology of Women*, Deutsch stated that "a mature woman without children is the psychologi-cal equivalent of a man without a male organ."

Imagine what they would have called a woman who wanted to be a Senator!

Sociologist Barbara Sinclair Deckard writes of magazine articles entitled, "Feminology Begins at Home," "Have Babies While You're Young," and "How to Snare A Male." She points out that one-third of the pictorial heroines in magazines in the '50s had careers, but "they were always psychologically sick and unhappy until they gave it up for the home." By 1959 there were no heroines with careers in magazines, "only happy housewives."

What I find interesting about Deckard's report is that all the while more and more women were going into the workplace. The reality was totally different from what was portrayed in the media. Deckard says, "In 1940, 25% of women were in the workforce; in 1945, 36% were in the workforce. After the war that percentage dropped to 29% but by 1960 about 38% of all women over the age of 16 were employed."

At the same time, the most widely quoted Freudian-based book, *Modern Women: The Lost Sex* by Farnham and Lunberg, said that early women's liberation leaders were sex starved and wanted to castrate all males and that "feminism was at the core a deep illness." They actually wrote that the more educated a woman, the more sexually dysfunctional she is. They recommended that women be barred from many occupations and that the government should pay for treatment of all neurotics "infected" by women's liberation.

When I graduated from high school in 1958, I had taken on the establishment in a small way because I decided to be an economics major, rather than a home economics major in college. According to Deckard, the former president of Mills College for Women, in California, said he would not include courses in which men are "naturally" better, like the sciences. He pushed food and nutrition, textiles, clothing, health and nursing, house planning and interior decoration, garden design and applied botany and child development.

As I entered Brooklyn College in 1958 as one of about three women to major in economics out of hundreds and hundreds of women, many of my classmates' moms were in the workplace, but in "women's jobs," usually at low pay, viewed as "helpers" and easily fired. They were telephone operators and teachers and nurses and librarians. Six percent of those listed in *Who's Who* in 1930 were women; only four percent were women in 1970. The glass ceiling was more like a cement ceiling in the 1950s.

I married in 1962 and worked until I had my first child in 1965. I had a hectic life and a good life—but I heard the voices of the women's movement through it all. And although I knew none of the sociology that I write about today, I knew those voices made sense.

Betty Friedan wrote in 1963 in her book *The Feminine Mystique*, "The problem that has no name—which is simply the fact that American women are kept from growing to their full human capacities—is taking a far greater toll on the physical and mental health of our country than any known disease." And she asked,"Who knows what women can be when they are finally free to become themselves?"

The '90s Model of Women

Voices like Friedan's pointed out that America was wasting its talent, that women could do more, that we should care about each other, that we could live up to our potential if we stopped setting limits on ourselves and each other, that we could work at decent jobs if we wanted to, or not work at all if we didn't want to or have to. I like the word liberation—it means freedom to be me. Being a feminist means being free to follow my dreams and to work so that others—men and women—have that same opportunity.

In 1992, women following their dreams to the United States Senate were not considered neurotic. Voters were unhappy with the economy, with the education system, with the domestic agenda, with homelessness, with health care, with the trade situation that saw our trading partners eating our lunch while the Republican Administration talked about fair trade and did virtually nothing to ensure it.

And then the people made a leap. They thought about their government and what it looked like. Every day, they saw George Bush surrounded by people who looked like him. And during the Hill-Thomas hearings, they saw the United States Senate—and it looked just like the people who surrounded George Bush. And the light bulb went on in America. If change was what we wanted, we had a way to do it. We could elect women to the Senate. We could even elect two from California, something unthinkable when Dianne Feinstein and I first decided to run for the two Senate seats that were up at the same time.

When we were on the campaign trail, the pundits and the pollsters always asked Dianne and me how we ever expected that both of us would get elected. "You're women," they would say; "You're both from Northern California"; and finally the zinger: "And you're both Jewish!" Many times I had asked them in reply if they had ever wondered how two white, Protestant males could get elected from the same state. That took them aback for a moment. It's a way to deal with prejudice and I highly recommend it—you just turn it around. "And besides," I would say, "the Senate could use a good dose of chicken soup."

So while the pundits were predicting doom and gloom for two women, Dianne and I knew that our joint election was possible, because when we were campaigning, the biggest roar always came when one of us said, "We can double the number of women in the Senate just from California—if Boxer and Feinstein win."

Dianne and I had never been close. We had always moved within different coalitions within the Democratic party in California. The press kept waiting for us to turn on each other—and they still are. They write stories comparing our poll ratings, which I've never seen done for two male Senators from the same state; they write stories that treat us as though we are joined at the hip. And when we differ they act like it's a big deal.

They don't understand that even though we have very different personalities, and disagree on occasion, we share a real respect and admiration for each other that comes from what we went through together—the most grueling campaigns imaginable. And there is also the very strong sense that we must be a team for California, a state that is in a very tough economic transition as we downsize our military. In addition, we have made history as the first two female Senators the state has ever had and only the 18th and 19th women in the entire history of the United States Senate.

When I was growing up, it was "common knowledge" that women didn't like each other, were jealous of each other and wanted each other to fail. Dianne and I remember those predjudices. But when I was dropping in the polls due to a very effective negative TV blitz in the general election, it was Dianne who came to my side. She didn't have to do it, because her vote was solid, and she eventually won in a landslide. She did it to help me, and she did it for California, and I will never forget her help when I needed it most. Whatever disagreements we have pale in light of what pulls us together.

1972 vs. 1992: A Study in Contrasts

In 1992 the California crowds roared at the possibility of two women Senators; in 1972 you never mentioned being a woman. You never brought it up, and you hoped nobody noticed.

The stories of those days are almost unimaginable to today's young women, but they should be told. It is important to realize where we were yesterday, so we understand where we are today and ensure that we won't step backward tomorrow.

When I decided to run for County Supervisor in 1971, I started doing what you do in every campaign. You line up support one voter at a time. In those days you put the name of each supporter on an index card and into a file box. On each card were special notes that told you if your supporter would volunteer, have a coffee klatch for you, do research or walk a precinct. Today we do the same thing with all the fancy computers. Personally, I yearn for the days of the old file box that I could watch grow every day. (Of course, I also yearn for the days when we had index cards for every book in the library instead of microfiche, but that's another topic.)

In 1971 one of the first people I went to see was my next-door neighbor. She was a well-respected teacher and a cordial neighbor, and I was excited to tell her my plans. She invited me in and we sat in her kitchen over a cup of coffee, like those warm, fuzzy coffee commercials. I put forward my explanation of the issues—preserving the beauty of our community and its humanity, making our county government more responsive and the county board meetings more open. I got more and more animated as I discussed the need to fight for the safety of our children as they crossed busy streets to get to school and the role the county should play in after-school activities to keep our kids out of trouble. I should have gotten an early clue from her silence that she was not going into the file box. Finally she said, "Barbara, I don't think you should do this. Your kids are young and it doesn't seem right."

I was stunned by her response. Here was a woman with a career, who loved her job and had two young children,

STRANGERS IN THE SENATE

just as I did. How could this be? For the first and only time in that campaign, I felt tears coming. I excused myself and went back to the house. Tears of rejection are tears I no longer cry because I have learned that rejection is a vital part of politics. Even if you are a very popular political figure, at any given time at least one of every three people is not thrilled with you.

I was lucky that I had to deal with rejection so early in my political career. I was lucky that I shed those tears early, because I had to answer a very serious question: Could I really take it? I was 32 years old and I was going to run for office. Was I going to grow up, or drop out?

I decided to grow up. I told myself then, as I tell myself now, so much so that it is a part of me, that when you break barriers you have to expect rejection and when you stand for something, you have to expect rejection. In politics today, you have to be ready for ridicule as well. You better believe in what you are doing, and you better hear lots of inner applause!

I convinced myself that had I gone over to my next door neighbor's house to tell her I was going to nursing school she would have cheered. But because I was trying for a job traditionally held by men, even though the men in local government had families and even outside jobs, I simply had to expect this kind of prejudice. And I faced more prejudice—the kind Pat Schroeder was using her sense of humor to fight in Denver.

There were days when I thought I had broken through, days when no one asked me how old my children were or what my husband thought of my candidacy. But then the prejudice would return.

I will never forget a luncheon held at a community hall in a beautiful part of the supervisorial district. The room was packed, and I took it as a great sign; you can't win them over if they aren't there. That afternoon the topic was preserving the hillsides. The community was willing to accept its share of growth but not in the hills. I agreed. This was a meeting of the minds, and, I hoped, a getting of the votes. My presentation went better than usual, as I went through the intricate planning issues of the county, which included transportation, flood control and density questions. I felt I was weaving my points together well.

This was an important audience—roughly 200 women who always voted. This had been strong territory for the incumbent who, though a nice guy, and a decent vote, could have been stronger on the environment in terms of his leadership. The environment was my "wedge" issue, as the pundits say today, meaning that I could drive a wedge between the voters and my opponent on the environment. And as I spoke, I watched the women nodding. I felt they were with me.

After I finished my presentation I asked for questions. A hand shot up in the back of the room so enthusiastically that I was extremely pleased—until she spoke.

"So, tell me, Barbara," she said. "When do you have time to do your dishes?"

I was stunned. Even though I knew it was a tough crowd—older women who didn't have careers and probably didn't understand my wanting one—I really thought I had gotten them to stop thinking about my gender by showing my concern for their community and the issues they cared about. But now I had to answer this irrelevant question, which was being asked in all seriousness. Trying the Schroeder approach, I used humor. "We use paper plates," I said. No one laughed.

Later, I thought I had made matters worse—first, by not "defending" myself and assuring them of the fact that my family life was under control, and second, by telling an environmental crowd that I used paper plates! The question ruined my rhythm and my day back in 1972, but when in 1992 my husband publicly joked that when I designed my dream house it didn't have a kitchen, I got elected to the United States Senate.

In 1972 children were constantly raised as a negative issue. There were letters to the editor asking who would watch them if I got elected to this part-time job. In 1992 Patty Murray got elected to the U.S. Senate as "a mom in tennis shoes."

In 1972 I walked what is known in the trade as "door to door." It's a hard thing, but a good thing to do when you're running for local office, even though I never understood why someone would vote for you simply because you ring their doorbell.

Well, not *everyone* votes for you because you knock on their door. One of these "no" votes came from a woman whose distress at my running I will never forget.

"Who's there?" she said.

"Barbara Boxer. I'm running for Supervisor."

The door opened and she said, "I didn't think you'd be so short!" (I still get that. People say I look large in newspaper photographs or TV. I think they can't imagine a petite woman in a man's arena. The irony is that Senators Mikulski, Murray, Kassebaum and Boxer are all about five feet tall!)

So after I disappointed this woman with my height—or rather lack of it—she said, "Oh . . . you're the one with four kids under school age, right?"

"No," I replied, hoping to get to the issues. "I have two children." I thought this would bring her a sense of relief, since she appeared very agitated. Instead she chose to argue with me.

"Oh no, you have four kids. They told me," she said.

At this point I knew I couldn't get this woman's vote if I had bare-handedly stopped a guided missile that was headed toward her house. So I told her, "Lady, giving birth is something you never forget, and I only did it twice!" The door slammed. She probably thought I left two of my children in the woods, without bread crumbs.

I will say that on election night in November, 1972 it was my seven-year-old son who kept me sane. After I lost a very close race, I phoned my son to talk to him early the next morning. He had spent the night with his aunt and uncle. I was fearful that the children might taunt him about his mom losing. (At age five, I didn't think my daughter would get anything like that.)

When he came on the phone, I gave him a carefully rehearsed speech. "Doug," I said, "Mommy tried to win an election, but lost by a little bit. If anyone says anything about it, don't you worry. It's all okay."

There were a few seconds of silence as I wondered what kind of trauma I had visited on this child. Then came these words of hope, which I shall never forget: "Mom, can you make me a peanut butter and jelly sandwich for lunch today?"

Thank God for kids! Contrary to what the psychiatrists of the '50s would have said, without mine I would never have been a United States Senator.

Chapter Five

A Brief History of Women in the Senate

To understand where we're going as women in the political arena, it's important that we take a little time to look
back. If you have spent any time in Washington, D.C. and
wandered around the great halls of the Capitol, you know
how difficult it is to imagine what the first woman Senator
to enter that beautiful chamber must have been thinking.

Women in America were not allowed to vote until 1920,
when the 19th Amendment to the Constitution was
passed. Since then, only 19 women have had the distinc-
tion of serving in the Senate. Before 1992, the "Year of the
Woman," only five women had ever been elected to serve
in the Senate in their own right, although a few others got
there in a variety of ways, and for short periods of time.

Of the 19 women Senators, for example, two were never
sworn in because Congress was not in session between

their election and the expiration of their terms. Another woman sat in the Senate for only one day, hardly enough time to make an impact—unless it had been on a day on which war was declared. But it wasn't. A number of women were appointed or elected to fill unexpired terms and served in the Senate for less than a year.

In an article entitled "Over His Dead Body: A Positive Perspective on Widows in the United States Congress," historian Diane Kincaid notes that most women have made their way to Congress via the so-called "widow's mandate," the practice by which the widow of a deceased member is awarded his seat to keep it "safe" until the next general election. The "widow's mandate" provided the opening for 70 percent of women Senators, before 1992. "Shattering the glass ceiling" was only possible for a woman when a man dropped dead on the floor!

It's different now. Today, every female Senator has made it up the Senate steps on her own. Only Senator Nancy Kassebaum of Kansas, a very well-respected Republican Senator, comes from a political family, her father being Alf Landon, a Senator and later a Republican nominee for President.

I think it is interesting to look at some female Senators, who, despite being widows or appointees, helped pave the way for the truly independent women Senators of today.

Senator Felton of Georgia

The first woman Senator was Democrat Rebecca Felton, who was appointed by the governor of Georgia, in 1922, two years after women got the vote. Felton holds three Senate records. She was the first woman Senator, she only served for one day, and at the age of 87, she was the oldest person ever to be sworn in.

(Which reminds me of a story about South Carolina Republican Senator Strom Thurmond, who at 91 is the oldest Senator ever. During the 1993 State of the Union Address, Senator Thurmond noticed a cluster of female Democratic Senators. He approached me and asked: "How many gals do you have on that side of the aisle?" "Five," I answered. "How many do we have on our side of the aisle?" he continued. "One," I answered. "Well," he said, "we got to get ourselves some more gals!" Not long after, Texas elected Kay Baily Hutchenson to the Senate to fill the seat vacated when Lloyd Bentsen was selected to be Treasury Secretary.)

Back in 1922, although many newspapers praised Mrs. Felton as a woman of exceptional character, some editors questioned the governor's motives in appointing her. They called the appointment "merely a pretty sentiment... an empty gesture." The *Pittsburgh Gazette-Times* stated, "He did not appoint a woman because he has respect for women in politics, but actually to smooth his own path to the Senate." In fact, the path was not to be smooth for Felton, but she made the most of her historic situation.

As described by Senator Robert Byrd in the *Congressional Record* in January 1985, Mrs. Felton went to Washington by train, in November of 1922, wondering about the reception that awaited her in the Capitol. How would the members of the Senate's 67th Congress react toward her? Would Senators oppose her taking the oath of office because of the precedent it would set? Or would the *Atlanta Journal*'s quote of a Republican that "it will be a brave man who objects," be correct?

Byrd went on to explain what occurred that day. Vice President Calvin Coolidge gaveled the Senators to order at noon on November 20, 1922. Rebecca Felton had arrived more than an hour earlier. "There were cheers from the women crowding the galleries as she took an empty seat.

But the Senate adjourned after only 12 minutes out of respect for the deceased Tom Watson, whose seat Felton would fill."

Mrs. Felton was back the next day and the galleries were again packed with women wearing the colors of their various feminist-rights groups. With women having gained the right to vote, even a woman Senator-for-a-day was a sight to behold after 143 years of an all-male Senate. As she walked down the aisle to occupy Watson's vacant seat, Felton turned, and according to reports, became the first Senator ever to blow onlookers a kiss.

After three other new Senators were sworn in, senior Georgia Senator William Harris stated Felton's case and hoped that there would be no objections. Just as Harris finished, Thomas Walsh of Montana rose to say that he didn't oppose Mrs. Felton personally, but objected to the "irregularity" of her seating. Just as Walsh was to speak further against her seating, a message came from the House that the President was ready to address a joint session of Congress. Mrs. Felton went along with the rest of the Senators and then returned to the Senate chamber to await her swearing-in.

Her "I do," as she swore to uphold the Constitution, was loud and clear. The president pro tempore chose to ignore the Senate rule forbidding outbursts from the gallery as the women present, as well as many of the Senators on the floor, broke into applause. (That also happened in 1992 when the Senators took their oaths of office—new batches of colorful suits mingling with the usual blues and grays on the Senate floor. Mrs. Felton wore a long black dress.)

The following day, Senator Felton proudly answered the roll call, then rose as the "junior Senator from Georgia." After thanking her colleagues, she said, " . . . [W]hen the women of the country come in and sit with you, though there may be but a very few in the next few years, I pledge to you that you will get ability, you will get integrity of purpose, you will get exalted patriotism, and you will get unstinted usefulness." With that, her Senate career ended, because the Senate term of her deceased predecessor expired in one day. However, Rebecca Felton used her moment in the sun to speak out for the right of women to serve in the Senate.

Senator Caraway of Arkansas

Rebecca Felton was right that more women would follow her into the Senate and that they would be women of quality. Unfortunately, she was also correct in saying that their numbers would be few.

Nearly ten years would go by before the next woman would be sworn into the Senate. Her name was Hattie Caraway, from Arkansas, and she was sworn in on December 9, 1931.

Senator Byrd shares her story with us as well as that of the other women Senators. In the journal she kept while a Senator, Mrs. Caraway noted that she had been given the same desk used by Rebecca Felton for her one day in the Senate. "I guess," she wrote, "they wanted as few of them contaminated as possible!" One quality that seems to connect all women Senators is their ability to laugh at themselves.

Although her Senate career followed that of her deceased husband, Mrs. Caraway accomplished many Senate "firsts" for women. In addition to being the first woman elected to the Senate (she ran in her own right in 1932), she was also the first woman to vote in the Senate, to preside over the Senate, to chair a Senate committee, and to preside over Senate hearings.

Hattie Caraway was appointed to fulfill the unexpired term of her late husband, Thad Caraway, who died suddenly of a heart attack. His death left Arkansas politicians with a messy problem. Had Thad Caraway died three days later, leaving less than a year until the next general election, the governor could have simply appointed someone to serve out the remainder of the term. But since he died leaving more than a year, an immediate appointment was necessary, to be followed by a special election.

In Arkansas in 1931, many candidates were considered to fill Caraway's Senate term, but all were more interested in the full six-year term up for grabs in the general election about a year away than in a single-year appointment. All agreed with the governor that naming Thad Caraway's widow as the interim appointee as well as the Democratic candidate in the special election for the remaining year would be the safest route to follow. They assumed that Mrs. Caraway had no interest in running for the full term—and they all learned a lesson. *Never* assume anything in politics. Hattie Caraway took the appointment, returned to Washington a grieving widow, and on December 9, 1931, was sworn in to the Senate. Then, on May 10, 1932, she filed for the full six-year term, shocking everyone.

Arkansas newspapers headlines reported that day, "Bombshell Explodes in Arkansas Politics," and "Senator Springs Surprise by Announcing for Office." But the seven male candidates who had filed didn't see Caraway as a threat. (Sixty years later I was viewed in the same way by my male opponents in the primary. They were my friends, but they underestimated my candidacy—the same way the candidacies of most female Senators were underestimated. This should no longer be the case for women who run for the United States Senate from now on.)

In 1932 Hattie Caraway had no campaign funds and no campaign manager, but her opponents became concerned, when in July, popular Senator Huey Long of Louisiana campaigned for Caraway in Arkansas. Long called Caraway the "little widow woman" who was "the true heir to the egalitarian philosophy" of her late husband. "We've got to pull a lot of pot-bellied politicians off a little woman's neck," he said, and Hattie Caraway made history by becoming the first woman ever elected to the United States Senate.

For the next six years Hattie Caraway devoted herself to her work. She made few public statements, but seeking to help her depression-stricken state, strongly supported almost all of President Franklin Roosevelt's New Deal legislation.

In her first official act as Senator, Mrs. Caraway inserted into the *Congressional Record* a radio address on the subject of "Youth in Politics and the Democratic Party," to emphasize the importance of participation in the political process by college students and young people across the nation. "The political activity and participation of young undergraduates has not kept pace with the activity or interest of students in the rest of the world . . . ," she noted. (Sixty years later, the women candidates all addressed the need for youth involvement. Very often I would say: "If the 20-somethings and the 30-somethings don't get involved, I will never win!" I spent a great deal of time addressing students.)

In 1938, Caraway was elected to her second term in the Senate. With the support of labor, veterans' and women's groups, she defeated Representative John McClellan by 8,000 votes. His slogan was "Arkansas needs another man in the Senate." In Senator Caraway's second term she continued to be one of President Roosevelt's most reliable supporters.

In 1943, Mrs. Caraway became a co-sponsor of the proposed Equal Rights Amendment to the Constitution, the first woman member of Congress to endorse it. Perhaps it was that co-sponsorship that led to her later defeat for a third term. But Hattie Caraway was a principled prelude of things to come.

Senator Long of Louisiana

In February 1936, another "first" for women occurred in the Senate when Senator Rose McConnel Long of Louisiana was sworn in, bringing the number of women in the Senate to two for the first time. Unfortunately, this record wasn't broken until 1992, when the historic number was increased to six.

Mrs. Long came to the Senate on the heels of tragedy when her husband, Senator Huey Long, was assassinated in the Louisiana state capitol building. Senator Hattie Caraway, who owed much of her success to the support given by Mrs. Long's husband, said, "It will be nice to have a woman's company in the Senate." (Fifty-six years later, Senator Barbara Mikulski was to say, "I've been looking out the window waiting for some Democratic women Senators.")

The charismatic Huey Long was a hard act to follow. Mrs. Long plunged into her committee work. She was appointed to five committees in the Senate, but her most effective work was on Public Lands and Surveys Committee, where she led the fight to enlarge Chalmette National Historical Park. (I predict women in the Senate will lead the fight for the environment.)

Senator Graves of Alabama

Unfortunately, Mrs. Long must have felt like an outsider. Unlike Hattie Caraway, who would be elected in her own right, and unlike the great Congresswoman Lindy Boggs of Louisiana, who made her own stellar career after being elected to her husband's seat, Mrs. Long left Washington in 1937, without seeking her own term. Then in mid-1937, Dixie Bibb Graves, Democrat of Alabama, arrived as the focus of controversy. She had been appointed by her husband, who argued, "She has as good a heart and head as anybody."

Dixie Bibb Graves did have a very public life, having worked hard for the cause of women's suffrage. The *New York Times* wrote that she was a woman who was "at home with deep-sea fishing, a shotgun, a garden spade, or a silver ladle at the banquet table." The *Times* also credited her with drafting some of her husband's speeches and influencing his key decisions.

In the midst of the political firestorm, Mrs. Graves became a Senator. As a "freshman" Senator, Mrs. Graves was assigned a seat in the rear of the chamber. "I'm supposed to be seen, but certainly not heard," Mrs. Graves once told a radio audience—and she was telling the truth, as she chose not to run in the 1938 election.

On January 10, 1938, Dixie Bibb Graves filed the following farewell address:

> Mr. President and fellow members of the Senate, I feel that I cannot let this occasion pass without a word of appreciation to this body. It will be pleasing hereafter to remember these things; for "I was a stranger, and ye took me in." I had expected, of course, formal courtesy from such a group as this, but I was quite unprepared for the more than generous welcome you extended me, for you took me in as one of yourselves, and more than that no one could have asked. Ever since I came into the Senate I have been the recipient of every courtesy, not only on the part of the members of this body, but of every official of the Senate, from the highest to the

lowest. Every want was anticipated, my ignorance was shielded, my steps were guided.

I am grateful indeed, to my fellow woman Senator, a woman who, though she first came to the Senate by appointment, yet has made such a name for herself and for womanhood that her own people have honored her with election to this great office. I do devoutly hope that in time to come their example will be followed in other states.

I am happy to serve in the present Administration, Mr. President and fellow Senators, under the inspiring leadership of that man who, sitting quietly in the White House, keeps watch over his own, the American people; that man born to riches, who has ever felt the needs of the poor; who clothed in privilege, has passionately fought for social justice, who has given every strength of his great heart and mind to his people, the American people. We honor him, we cherish him today, but in that great tomorrow to which we all must come, I verily believe when that great judge of all compiles the roster of immortals, the name of Franklin Roosevelt will be enrolled as one who loved his fellow man.

I have been privileged, I have been honored, far beyond my deserts, far beyond any expectations I may have had, at serving at such a time and in such a group, and I verily believe that with your counsel, and the President's counsel, working together, all will be well with our beloved country.

It seems to me that America lost an elegant Senator when Dixie Bibb Graves decided not to run for a full term. It's a pity that many others like her were denied that opportunity—not by law but by custom and tradition.

Senator Smith of Maine

The first woman to serve in both the House and the Senate arrived in Washington in 1936, as the wife and secretary to Representative Clyde H. Smith of Maine. Margaret Chase Smith is probably the best known of the women Senators who served before the revolution of 1992. Her career began suddenly, in 1940, when her husband died and she won a special election to take his place in the House of Representatives.

Smith was a moderate Republican, who in 1960 attained the highest percentage of the vote of all Republican Senatorial candidates nationally. Her popularity soared when she attacked McCarthyism on the Senate floor. She later said:

> If I am to be remembered in history ... it will not be because of legislative accomplishments, but for an act I took as a legislator in the United States Senate when on June 1, 1950 I spoke in the Senate in condemnation of McCarthyism at a time when the then junior Senator from Wisconsin had the Senate paralyzed with fear that he would purge any Senator that disagreed with him.

Senator Smith was the first in her party to attack McCarthy for his politics of hate and fear. You can imagine the shock in the Senate when she said:

> I do not like the way the Senate has been made a rendez-vous for vilification, for selfish political gain at the sacrifice of individual reputations and national unity. . . . I do not want to see the party ride to political victory on the Four Horseman of Calumny—fear, ignorance, bigotry, and smear.

When asked by a reporter in the 1980s, about the difficulty of giving her declaration on McCarthyism, she said:

> Oh my! I'll say it was difficult! But someone had to do it. . . . I had been in the Senate only a year, and I had been on this investigating committee with McCarthy. The more I thought of it, the more I thought, someone has to do this.
>
> When [my assistant and I] walked over . . . we met Senator McCarthy and he said, "Margaret, what's the trouble? You look awfully glum this morning." I said, "I'm making a speech and you're not going to like it."

Margaret Chase Smith condemned McCarthy's tactics in front of the world. It defied the unwritten rules of party unity, but Margaret Chase Smith went on to become one of the most popular Senators ever, being reelected four times.

Her approach to campaigning was also trend-setting. She refused to accept campaign contributions, believing that she would feel obligated to please special interests. Years later, when asked by a *Los Angeles Times* reporter about her ability to campaign without big money donors she said:

> It must be remembered that this was a long time ago, and much has happened since my days. I did it because people supported me, because they believed in me. I didn't have paid campaign managers. I did not have paid people. People felt, as the Constitution says, that people are the government. . . . Of course I didn't have to buy much radio or television, because I was for a long time the only

woman. I, for one reason or another, was news—whatever I was doing. It wasn't necessary to buy time—or I didn't think it was.

Raising money was not on Margaret Chase Smith's list of priorities. Instead, she focused her attention on her work in the Senate, particularly in the area of military preparedness. (One could compare the efforts in the '50s of Margaret Chase Smith in the area of military reform to those made by Representative Pat Schroeder today. Both have been spokeswomen for women serving in the military.) Margaret Chase Smith earned the nickname "Mother of the Waves" after introducing legislation to establish the women's branch of the Navy.

"I never was a woman candidate. I never was a woman Senator or Representative—I was one of them. Perhaps I was different. Perhaps I came in at a different time. I'm not sure about that. But I think too much emphasis is placed on 'I'm only a woman,' " Senator Smith said. (I agree with Margaret Chase Smith that gender alone does not a great person make, but I also think that it's not healthy for an institution that is supposed to be of, for, and by the people to be of, for, and by only half of the people.)

In 1972, the long reign of the "Lady of Maine" ended. She was defeated in her fifth run for the United States Senate, after 24 years of service in the highest legislative body in the land—justifiably proud of her perfect attendance record. Upon leaving the Senate, she said, "I hate to leave the Senate when there is no indication another qualified woman is coming in. We've built a place here for quality service. If I leave and there's a long lapse, the next woman will have to rebuild entirely."

Like many people of her time, Margaret Chase Smith thought in terms of "one woman" at a time in the U.S. Senate. That philosophy of tokenism has held for a long time—one reason why it's so important that there are now seven women in the Senate and two women on the Supreme Court.

Rebuilding the Senate for women has been a long, arduous process. Eight other women served in the Senate since the election of Margaret Chase Smith until the revolution of 1992. As with earlier Senators, many of the women to serve got there by way of "the widow's mandate."

Senator Bowring of Nebraska

In 1954 along came Mrs. Eva Bowring, appointed to fill out the term of Senator Dwight Griswald, Republican of Nebraska. In addition to a long career in Republican party work, Mrs. Bowring was well known for joining her ranch hands whenever they needed her, even when it meant riding through blizzards to rescue stray cattle from freezing on the open range.

At a press conference to accept the open seat, Mrs. Bowring said, "I'm going home to kiss the cattle goodbye." She would then head off to Washington to become the 13th woman Senator ever to serve. However, she didn't consider the number 13 to be an evil omen. "Prepare yourself," she said, "there will be more women."

Senator Abel of Nebraska

Senator Bowring served only six months in the Senate before rejoining her beloved cattle. For the first time in history, however, one woman Senator succeeded another! Since Mrs. Bowring retired before the end of her term, a special election was held to fill out the two remaining months of the term. Mrs. Hazel Abel campaigned hard and won. Upon her victory, she said, "To me, it was more than a short term in the Senate. I wanted Nebraska voters to express their approval of a woman in government."

Senator Abel's first vote on November 8, 1954 was to condemn Senator Joe McCarthy's conduct. Clearly, the women in the Senate would stand up to the politics of fear.

Senators Neurenburger, Edwards, Humphreys, and Allen

Two women served out the remaining terms of their deceased predecessors. One, Senator Maurine Neurenburger of Oregon, was appointed to fill out her husband's term. The other, Elaine Edwards, was appointed by her husband, the governor of Louisiana, to fill out the term of the late Senator Allen J. Ellender. Both served less than a full term and neither sought re-election.

After Senator Edwards resigned in 1972, and Margaret Chase Smith left the Senate in January of 1973, another five years passed before another woman, soon joined by a second, sat in the Senate. Both joined the ranks of the Senate via the "widow's mandate." In 1978, Muriel Humphrey arrived to serve out the term of her husband, Herbert Humphrey of Minnesota. And Maryon Allen served out the term of her husband, James.

Senator Kassebaum of Kansas

In 1978, the first woman elected to fill a full Senate term without having been a widow of a member of Congress took office. Her name was Nancy Kassebaum, Republican of Kansas. The daughter of a very famous father—1936 Republican Presidential candidate Alf Landon—Nancy Kassebaum began her own political life when she went to work as a legislative aide to Senator James Pearson of Kansas in 1975.

When Senator Pearson announced his retirement in 1978, Kassebaum was dissuaded from running for a Congressional seat and decided to run for Pearson's soon-to-be-vacant seat instead. With the support of her family, especially her mother, Kassebaum ran on the slogan, "Nancy Landon Kassebaum: A Fresh Face, a Trusted Kansas Name," and defeated eight opponents in the primary and three (male) opponents in the general election.

Nancy Kassebaum has established herself as one of the most popular Senators in state history and continues to fight for her constituents today. They, in turn, have re-elected her twice—apparently choosing to ignore her earlier pledge to quit after two terms!

Senator Hawkins of Florida

In 1980, the year of the Reagan landslide, the first woman from Florida was elected to the Senate: Paula Hawkins, who used her "housewife" image in her Senatorial campaign as the Republican candidate to narrowly defeat her conservative Democratic opponent.

She said, "It is a tremendous advantage being a woman in government . . . most of us still stay in touch with reality—I go [to] buy groceries at midnight. Most people in Washington are so isolated by their staffs [that] they are isolated from the world. You need to rub shoulders with the people."

Hawkins burst onto the national scene by confronting a very serious issue in America today. Very bravely, she revealed herself to the nation, and spoke of her own experience of being sexually abused as a child. She was able to effectively bring the issue to national prominence by disclosing her own story, thus inspiring others to deal with the issue of sexual abuse. In 1986 Paula Hawkins was defeated in her bid for reelection.

Senator Mikulski of Maryland

In that year, Barbara Mikulski of Maryland made Democratic history.

She incorporated being a woman into her campaign, she incorporated being a woman into her legislative program, and she took the slings and arrows of being the first self-described feminist to be elected in her own right to the United States Senate.

Chapter Six

Senator Barbara Mikulski: The Promise of Things to Come

On Monday, July 13, 1992 Senator Barbara Mikulski, the first Democratic woman elected to the U.S. Senate on her own, right from the start, approached the podium at the Democratic National Convention in New York.

Bill Clinton and Al Gore would be officially nominated later that week and would speak from the same podium. But on July 13, history would be made—because for the very first time in history, six Democratic women had already won their party's nomination. That night, they would address the convention in a 30-minute block.

"Women's Night" was Democratic Party Chairman (now Commerce Secretary) Ron Brown's idea, and I thought it was a good one. I also remember that the logistics were controversial because, except for Senator Mikulski, the rest of us were to address the crowd from the convention floor on raised platforms. There was some grumbling about this, on the order of, "Men would never speak except from the main stage, so why are the women not on the main stage?" I myself felt very comfortable standing "with the people."

Standing at my raised platform in the middle of the convention floor, I had a bird's-eye view of my friend, the Senator from Maryland. I remembered sitting in her office a few years earlier, seeking her advice on my political future. She and I had always worked well together in the House of Representatives.

A Political Mentor

When I went to see Barbara in 1989, it was to get a sense of whether the U.S. Senate would give me the opportunity to do more for my state and whether I would like working in the U.S. Senate—if I could ever pull off a victory. At that time anyone asked if I could win would have answered that a couch had a better chance of becoming a U.S. Senator than I did.

Mikulski got right to the point.

"How old are you, Babs?"

"Almost 50," I said.

"Well if you're ready to leave the House of Representatives, and never look back, and never regret, then I'd say 50 is the perfect time.

"You can do more here, you can be heard here, and it's worth the fight you'll have to wage to get here. And it will be a fight," she warned. "Of course," she said with that Mikulski twinkle, "you could do it for me. I need someone to look in the eye!"

Barbara Mikulski and I have a lot in common. In addition to our under-five-foot stature, we both started our careers in local government, went on to serve ten years in the House of Representatives, and ran for the Senate at the age of 50.

Humor: An Essential Asset

Mikulski and I also believe that a sense of humor can win the day. Hers is legendary and pops up at the most unexpected moments. When asked by *Glamour* how she felt about being named *Glamour*'s Woman of the Year, along with the singer Madonna, Mikulski, who is not known for being glamorous, replied, "She's got her assets, I've got mine, and we both make the best use of what God has given us." (Mikulski's award was for her contribution to women's health issues, which she continues to champion on a daily basis.)

When discussing the problems of being a woman in politics, Mikulski explains, "If you're married, you're neglecting him; if you're single, you couldn't get him; if you're divorced, you couldn't keep him; and if you're widowed, you killed him!" When she recited that litany to a huge group of women parliamentarians from all over the world, there was a dead silence and she thought to herself, "My God, I've gone too far!" But then, she says, "those little translations in their ears caught up, and the women all stood up and gave me a standing ovation."

Mikulski's sense of humor comes quite naturally, and she says she finds it defuses the tension which can often dominate political life. I learned that same lesson early and I think that women in particular can break the ice with a sense of humor.

When I got to the House of Representatives in 1983, I was shocked to hear that women members of Congress couldn't use the gym. As a Californian, I knew the value of exercise, and at the time I was a faithful aerobiciser and had gotten accustomed to working out in a gym at least three times a week. When I complained, I was told there was a "Ladies Gym." Although I had my doubts about "separate but equal" facilities I decided, at that point, not to kick up a fuss. I was new and I didn't want my male colleagues to get too stunned too fast. But *I* was the one who was stunned. Pat Schroeder had described the women's gym as a "3 by 5" room with five old-fashioned hooded hair dryers and a ping-pong table—and she was right!

Undeterred, I decided to organize an aerobics class for the women members of Congress. My longtime friend Claudette Josephson led the class. In walked Geraldine Ferraro of New York, Barbara Kennelley of Connecticut, Olympia Snow of Maine, Barbara Mikulski and me.

Except for Claudette and me, the entire group was from the East Coast; in 1983, most Easterners thought we Californians were a bit nuts when it came to exercise. But I had prevailed upon them and they came—all in workout outfits that I would have worn out to dinner in California. (In the East, this was as casual as they would get.)

The class started. Claudette said, "Let's stretch on the floor." Groans. She said, "Stand up and we'll stretch our arms, way up." Groans. "Put your hands on your hips." Groans. "Now, bend from the waist."

Suddenly, Mikulski couldn't take it anymore. "If I had a waist, I wouldn't be here," she bellowed.

That was the end. We were all laughing so hard we couldn't stop.

The room we were in was so small we couldn't do much anyway. Claudette got through about 15 minutes of the class and everyone started bowing out, thinking, I am sure, that they would never try this again. As for me, I realized I needed to get into the main gym to use the machines. Hair dryers and a ping-pong table simply did me no good.

The story of the integration of the Congressional gym shows how a sense of humor can help. I knew I needed help, so in my second term, I lined up seven male members to assist me—the younger ones whose wives worked out and who understood that if it was important for a male member to stay in decent shape it was just as important for a female member to do so. George Miller, Marty Russo, Tom Downey and Dick Durbin became my behind-the-scenes advisors and tried to calm the waters of the "gym committee."

Unfortunately for me, the "gym committee" was composed of older members who weren't exactly sympathetic. We tried everything, to no avail. Then I hit on it—use a sense of humor.

At that time, Congresswomen Mary Rose Oakar, Marcy Kaptur and I had formed a little singing group. We wrote funny words to songs and entertained at political fund-raisers and parties. For example, we sang to the tune of "The Way We Were":

> *Memories—of the days before Phil Gramm*
> *Happy, DEM-O-CRAT-IC memories*
> *Of the way we were . . .*
> *There was transit, there was housing, student loans...*

You get the picture!

Here's how we broke through to the gym.

To the tune of "Has Anyone Seen My Girl?" Mary Rose, Marcy and I sang to our colleagues:

Exercise / Glamorize
Where to go / Will you advise
Can't everybody use your gym?
Equal Rights / We'll wear tights
Let's avoid those macho fights
Can't everybody use your gym?
We're not trim / We're not slim
Can't you make it hers and him?
Can't everybody use your gym?

I remember that my California colleague Tony Cohelo thought it was so funny that he asked us to sing at a Congressional whips meeting.

We did. And guess what? We got into the gym.

My mother always said, "Ask nicely the first time, and if that doesn't work, ask nicely the second time." This was my second time and I was nice and it worked.

Now it's no big deal. The women in the House now are much younger and there are more of them, so they will probably use the gym more. Now they need to get a decent locker room and bathroom on the same floor as the gym. I've got a tune in mind, to: "Thanks for the Memories."

Thanks for the locker room
We're working out again
But since we sweat like men . . .

On second thought, I hope they'll just ask. Working out is not really a laughing matter. It's a necessity for everyone, particularly those of us in stressful, 12-to-15 hour-a-day jobs!

Women In the Senate: Looking Forward

But Mikulski was right when by example she taught me to keep that sense of humor going.

I waited for that Mikulski sense of humor in Madison Square Garden. I was halfway to my U.S. Senate goal. Just as Mikulski had defied the odds in 1986 in defeating a very qualified array of male office holders in her Senate primary, so had I. We were little women but big risk-takers.

I relished hearing Mikulski's words on that July night because I knew her speech would be moving, straightforward, and to the point. I knew she would connect with real people as she always does, and I knew she would use her sense of humor. She said:

> We Democratic women . . . will change the U.S. Senate fundamentally and forever. There will be a new vitality, a new heart, a new spirit and a new way of doing business. A woman is not amazed to find that there are electric scanners in the grocery store [a reference to George Bush's surprised reaction to scanners at a Washington, D.C. trade show] . . . she knows how to spell 'potato' because she buys them in a bag to stretch the family dollar [a reference to Dan Quayle's spelling bee faux pas]. . . .
>
> We women speak a different language. We will seek different results. We won't just talk about family values: we'll make sure a mom and dad can stay home from work when a child is sick. . . .
>
> And never again when a woman comes forward to tell her story to a committee of the United States Senate will she ever be assaulted for telling the truth.

The crowd went wild. There was Anita Hill again.

A Leader in the Senate

Mikulski says her darkest moments as a U.S. Senator came during the Thomas-Hill face-off.

As soon as Hill's charges hit the press Mikulski had tried from the inside to get a hearing. At first she was hit with a wall of indifference from the Senators. What distressed her more than anything, she said, was the failure of her male colleagues to understand that the issue was really about power—the power that Clarence Thomas had over his employee Anita Hill and the lack of power Anita Hill had in the situation. Amazingly, many male Senators viewed Thomas as the "victim" and didn't recognize the lack of power so many women feel in the workplace, she told me.

Senator Mikulski realized that her own ability to change her colleagues' attitudes was limited by her gender, so she went to some of her male counterparts who had been prosecutors. She asked them to explain to Senators who were reluctant to call a hearing, how the dynamics of male-female harassment worked, how women often fear coming forward or refuse to press charges and how the system turns on them.

Partly as a result of the efforts of Mikulski and her allies, Senate attitudes began to change a little. When the public outcry continued and they saw such things as "the march of the Congresswomen," the Senate reversed itself and the hearing was convened.

The hearings and the confirmation vote galvanized America, and many firms began to hold meetings and seminars about sexual harassment in the workplace. Mikulski made sure the Senate didn't forget the lessons of the Hill-Thomas debacle. She teamed up with then-Senator, now Vice President Al Gore, and the two hosted a series of dinner meetings with Senators and spouses in a "no-fault" atmosphere to discuss "The Dynamics of Gender." They brought in experts in communication between men and women to provide much-needed information. She felt it was crucial for her male colleagues to learn that women may well view things differently than men do. It doesn't mean that women have a "better" view, she says, just a different view.

Mikulski feels she owes a great deal to Al Gore for his interest in continuing the dialogue after the Thomas-Hill hearings. "If I had set up those meetings myself," she says, "they would have thought it was some kind of feminist plot, but with Gore's help, we pulled in a good number of Senators and spouses and they found it rewarding." Mikulski and Gore deserve a lot of credit for turning an otherwise disastrous hearing into an opportunity for remedying some serious problems.

Three years earlier, in 1988, Mikulski made another contribution to male-female communication in the Senate when she handled an infuriating situation so well that I believe male Senators will forever be deterred from publicly embarrassing female Senators.

One Saturday night in Washington, D.C., a Republican colleague of Mikulski's was giving one of those "humorous" speeches at a private club. Included in his remarks was a comment on how he didn't know what got into Barbara Mikulski one day. She just "threw her panties at me," he said.

The press wanted an immediate reaction. Mikulski's staff advised her to let it go. "You're doing so well in the Senate, getting so much done," they reasoned. "Just ignore it."

Mikulski disagreed. "If I let it go now," she said, "then I will always have to be silent if something like this comes up again. If I speak now, this kind of thing will stop."

But she also knew she had to get the incident behind her. Mikulski told the press: "I find his comments insulting and outrageous and I want an apology."

The Republican Senator, after being assured she would accept his apology, phoned Senator Mikulski. "I was just kidding, Barbara," he said. "It was all in fun."

Senator Mikulski replied: "If someone said that about your wife or daughter, wouldn't you be offended?"

"You're right," he said. "I'm deeply embarrassed." The two then put out a joint press release and it was over.

This may seem like a small issue, but it is not. By asserting her self-respect and demanding recognition of her dignity, Senator Mikulski sent a very clear signal to colleagues who were simply not used to working with women as equals: such behavior would no longer be accepted.

Barbara Mikulski really helped those of us who would join her in the Senate, and those who will join us, by not running away from an unpleasant incident. And then, by moving beyond it and putting it behind her, she showed her willingness to forget it and to work with her colleagues for the good of the institution and the country. Mikulski was forceful yet conciliatory. "You can go from high ground to carping very quickly in these kinds of incidents," she says. "You need to handle them carefully."

More Women in the Senate: The Future is Here

When you are pretty much alone, it isn't easy to step out and know what to do when faced with prejudice. That's why Barbara Mikulski was so hopeful as she addressed the Democratic Convention and considered the possibility of more women in the Senate.

"I believe," she said, "that the wave is just beginning to rise. I believe that soon our government will be made up of people of all races and that women in high office will never be a novelty again. I believe this year brings a message of great hope—hope created, barriers brought down, and doors pushed open by the American people, reclaiming their country and reclaiming their power."

And then she paused and looked out at us again:

> My heart swells with pride to know that I will no longer be the only Democratic woman in the United States Senate. I will be joined by a team of spectacular women . . . and by the way, I think there are a lot more on the way.

Senator Barbara Mikulski is a risk-taker, a committed community organizer, a problem solver, a champion of the working class—always underestimated by the experts—always loved by the people. She says she tries to make up for her petite size with "spunk, spirit and savvy." She has paved the way for many of us, not only as a model in the way she gets elected, but by her success in the United States Senate, where she chairs the Appropriations Subcommittee on VA-HUD-Independent Agencies, heads the Labor and Human Resources Subcommittee on Aging, and is Assistant Floor Leader.

She recalls her emotions when the four of us joined her in the U.S. Senate as colleagues—Feinstein, Boxer, Murray and Moseley-Braun. "It didn't hit me until I sat in the meeting of all Democratic Senators after the November '92 election. We were in the old Senate chambers, that beautiful, historic room and I heard the names—*Carol* Mosely-Braun, *Barbara* Boxer, *Dianne* Feinstein and *Patty* Murray—and it hit me: I didn't have to be the Democratic woman Senator 'at large' anymore. It wasn't that I felt isolated before, there were the Sir Gallahads—Sarbanes, Kennedy, Gore, Mitchell, Lautenberg and others—but I did feel lonely from time to time, because I did have this weight on my shoulders—a huge constituency of American women. I felt happy, relieved and moved."

Proud to Be a Woman Senator

Just as Geraldine Ferraro had shown that women can have the dignity, the poise, the temperament, and the intelligence to run for high executive office, Barbara Mikulski had done the same thing for women like me who aspired to the highest legislative body in the land.

She made history by being the first Democratic woman ever elected in her own right, but she was more than that.

She was the first woman in the Senate to embrace the term "feminist." She got elected as a fighter for the people; a first-generation no-nonsense Democrat, proud of her Polish ancestry and proud to be a Democrat! And when she was asked if she was a feminist, Mikulski said—without blinking an eye—"Absolutely," even though her base of support would not identify with the word.

Mikulski works for her Maryland constituency tirelessly but has never run away from the broader constituency of American women who looked to her to protect their equality, their rights, their health care, their dignity, and their hopes and dreams. For the women Democratic Senators now and in the future, she is our Jackie Robinson—our Rosa Parks.

She often speaks of her life before she was a Senator. "When I worked on the streets of Baltimore as a social worker, my supervisor told me I didn't have a therapeutic personality," she says. Years later, Mikulski joked that George Bush would certainly agree with that assessment as he and Mikulski clashed over priorities. But remembering those days, Mikulski says, "My personality wasn't that important to me. What was important was organizing people, giving them a sense of their own power."

Her first "public" effort was organizing her ethnic community and the African-American community in the 1970s. That had never been done before, but Mikulski quips, "I could do anything. After all I was prominent. My grandmother owned a Polish bakery!" The communities, united together for the first time, stopped the construction of an expressway that would have destroyed their neighborhoods.

Mikulski sees women in politics through her own personal experience:

> Most of the women that hold public office essentially
> ... don't come through the traditional routes of being
> in a nice law firm or belonging to the right club ...
> but go into politics because they see a wrong they
> want to right or a need that must be filled.

Mikulski told a gathering of the Democratic Senatorial Campaign Committee's Women's Council, "Some women stare out the window waiting for Prince Charming. I stare out the window waiting for more women Senators!" She says she already sees a difference with four new women there: "We don't approach our jobs like technocrats with green eye shades on. We speak to the day-to-day problems of people. . . . There's a new look, a new energy, that is confidence-building for the people of the country."

Since 1987, Mikulski has been a Senator pushing for a relevant domestic agenda for America's families. In that fight she has helped to elect more Democratic women to the Senate. As Chair of the Women's Council of the Democratic Senatorial Campaign Committee she proved that women could become a potent force in the male-dominated field of fundraising.

And now her wish for more Democratic female Senators has come true. "I'm proud to be the first Democratic woman ever elected to the Senate," she once said, "but I don't want to be the last."

She's not the last. She was the promise of things to come.

Chapter Seven

Behind the "Miracle" of 1992

I can't say that being elected to the United States Senate was the fulfillment of a life-long dream, because girls and young women were not really allowed that kind of dream when I was growing up. But I can say my election and the election of several other women to the Senate is the fulfillment of an American Dream previously reserved for American men.

More Than a Personal Victory

The election of one or two new women to the Senate represents personal and unique victories, but in 1992 there were four such victories—and a clear connection of one victory to another.

The connection was the clear domestic agenda we all shared, the strong verbalized feelings of sympathy for Anita Hill, a willingness to call ourselves feminists, and a strong fighting spirit for change. But with the exception of Senator Dianne Feinstein, who was clearly leading in the polls from the day she decided to run, the rest of us came from far behind in the primaries to win upset victories.

As a backdrop to the individual campaigns, the media was greatly playing up 1992 as "The Year of the Woman." Many stories and articles pointed out that "The Year of the Woman" had often been anticipated, but had fizzled in the past. Would it happen again? they asked, over and over again, documenting the fallen hopes of women in politics in past years. Every time a woman politician encountered a negative event in her campaign, stories about history repeating itself would appear. I soon began to realize that the Senate elections of 1992 were far bigger than those of us running.

The women's races began to take on the aspect of a referendum on women and women's issues, a referendum on new priorities and cuts in military spending and a referendum on the very electability of women. Subtle— and not so subtle—questions abounded. Could we close the gap in the polls? Did we have the stamina? Could we be tough enough? Could we raise the money? Could we take the heat?

And we took the heat. All of us.

The 1992 Campaign

In 1990, I sought out Senator Barbara Mikulski for advice. I'd served in the House of Representatives since 1983, and although I was proud of what I'd been able to accomplish there, I wanted to do more than I could as a House member. Furthermore, it looked as though 1992 was going to offer an unprecedented opportunity for any Californian who was thinking about running for the United States Senate. It looked like veteran Democratic Senator Alan Cranston might not run for reelection, thus creating an open seat for a full six-year term. As it turned out, the second Senate seat became available when then-Senator Pete Wilson became Governor Pete Wilson and there would be an election for that seat in 1992 as well.

After consulting with Senator Mikulski—and having a long talk with my husband Stew and my kids, I decided to enter the race for Cranston's seat.

A Bruising Primary

Of course, I wasn't the only Democrat who wanted Cranston's seat. So did several others, which meant there would be a primary fight. Although I had a solid record on which to run—I'd been active in local politics going back to the early '70s, and the voters of my district had elected me to the House of Representatives five times—the other candidates were fiercely competitive and able to raise enormous amounts of money.

As always, I was running for the office because of the issues. With such important issues as gun control, reproductive choice, preservation of the environment, and the conversion from a Cold War to a peacetime economy in the midst of a serious recession before us, I wanted to make sure that California voters knew where I stood—especially voters from outside my home district, who might not even have heard of me. So I started campaigning, certain that I could run a good race, that I could get my views out to the public.

Trial by Press

Now, campaigning has to qualify as one of life's most abnormal experiences—unless you are used to being abused. Especially in a state as big as California, which is larger than many of the world's nations, the pace is brutal, the distances you have to cover monumental. And with the pressures of raising money, trying to do the job you already hold, and dealing with an adversarial press, campaigns today are as tough as anything in life can be. Maybe we in America have somehow decided that our leaders must go through campaign hell in order to make sure that they don't crack under the pressure that they'll encounter in office.

As it happened, I came very close to dropping out of the U.S. Senate race during the primary campaign. I was campaigning non-stop in the Sacramento area three months before the June 1992 primary. I went up there with my newest stump speech, one that I had worked on for days. It laid out the issues clearly and concisely. I talked about my plans for jobs, for economic conversion, for a clean and healthy environment, for choice, for crime prevention and for children. I talked about the need to protect our wetlands and oceans and how we needed to get the special interest money out of politics. I had several opportunities to present it—to an audience of grassroots environmentalists, to a dinner of Democratic activists, and at a couple of small parties given in my honor.

After each speech the press gathered around. Their questions had nothing to do with the speech I had just given, nothing to do with the issues I would have to tackle in the Senate, nothing to do with the economy which was in the dumps. Instead, they asked about how I could possibly win this election.

I was down in the polls with only three months to go; my money wasn't coming in the way they thought it should; the lieutenant governor (the front-runner) was absolutely the clear favorite and my other opponent had a ton of money and was attacking me with negative ads. The revelations of the House Bank added to my opponents' arsenal of attacks and to the nastiness of the press.

The implication was that I had no business in the race. Added to all that was the theory espoused by many reporters and pundits, that there was no way in God's universe that Dianne Feinstein would lose.

Happily they were right about that, but they then made what they thought was the irrefutable leap that it was completely impossible for a woman to win the other Senate seat for which I was running.

Things began to get to me. I was flying back and forth from California to Washington, doing my very best to be in the House of Representatives for critical votes. If I missed a vote, one of my opponents would deride me; if I missed a campaign event, my supporters would be hurt, no matter what I tried to do to apologize; I couldn't seem to get into a liveable rhythm. The red-eye (the overnight flight to D.C. from California) became the rule rather than the exception and I couldn't shake the jet lag.

Sometimes I felt if I had to ask one more person for a campaign contribution I would choke; yet I was forced by my chief fundraisers Suone Cotner and Nancy Kirschner to sit in my Los Angeles headquarters, as candidates say, "dialing for dollars."

I hated it! I have absolutely no problem raising money for other candidates and other causes but it is so hard to figuratively get down on your hands and knees and beg for yourself.

This is the financing system that we have in America today for Congressional candidates, and it is a disgrace. On the other hand, once Presidential candidates win their nominations they get public financing raised through a voluntary income tax check-off.

I fought long and hard for reform of this system, and on May 25, 1993 I rose in support of Senator John Kerry's amendment to emulate the Presidential system in Senate races.

Sadly the amendment failed again, and once more Senate candidates will have to do what I did in my campaign and beg and cajole and convince contributors to help. In many ways I was lucky, because people responded favorably to my phone entreaties about 50 percent of the time.

My staff knew how much I hated "phone time" so they went out and bought a used, cozy couch on which I could cuddle up in my sweatsuit and at least be physically comfortable while I did what was the most unpleasant part of campaigning—the money chase.

So one day in March of 1992, just three months before the primary, I decided I didn't want it anymore, I didn't need it anymore, and I'd be happier doing something else.

On the way home from Sacramento, I phoned Stew and told him I was going to drop out of the race.

I really expected him to cheer. He was worried about me—the unbelievable pace I was keeping, the way I was looking. We both wanted to spend more time together, and had been rationalizing that "soon" our life would be more normal. I really thought he would encourage me to leave the race. Instead he said, "Let's talk about it when you get home."

After I made the phone call to Stew, I invited Katie and John of my staff for dinner at a roadside diner. I told them I wasn't going to continue, that I couldn't get my message out because the media didn't feel the people were interested in the issues but rather in polls and personal attacks. They didn't have one iota of interest in my detailed program for economic recovery or my vision of the new world order or my plan to get 25 percent of America's children out of poverty and despair. I would no longer have to put up with press conferences meticulously planned and arranged by a dedicated staff and excited endorsers and supporters but—no press!

Or on a good day—a very few.

Katie and John were stunned. They turned pale, then told me that I was tired and hot and not thinking clearly. But I was adamant and frankly, quite relieved. I really had decided to quit.

Moments of Truth

We had one more stop to go—a Democratic party dinner and just before it, a gathering of women to watch "60 Minutes," which was doing a story about EMILY's List, the incredible organization that has changed the face of politics by tapping the women of the country to help women candidates.

Surrounded by a huge group of women I had never met before, I sat down to watch the TV show. I was sad. This was an intolerable situation. I was sitting there as a candidate and I wanted to tell them that I was quitting, but obviously it wasn't the right time or place to do it. I'll hold a press conference tomorrow, I thought. Meanwhile I'll make believe I'm still a candidate.

It was quite a show.

"60 Minutes" focused on two female Senatorial candidates—Geraldine Ferraro and me. They showed the contributions pouring in for both of us and for Dianne Feinstein, too. They had a film clip of me during the early days in the campaign—when I was fresh and optimistic—not the way I felt that night. The video reflected the excitement of a campaign based on real issues. All the women watching with me were elated. "How can we join EMILY's List?" they wanted to know. "Barbara," one said, "we're so proud of you for your courage!"

I thought, If you only knew how wrong you are.

Pulling into the driveway at about 10 p.m., I said good night to my staff and went inside the house. Surprisingly, my children—Doug, a lawyer at 27, and Nicole, in the film business at 25—were there. What were they doing there? Both had hectic lives and had their own apartments in San Francisco.

I realized Stew must have called them, but to this day he won't discuss it. Anyway, there they were downstairs waiting for me; Stew was upstairs. I called up to him. "Let's have a family discussion about my dropping out." He yelled down that he was watching a ball game so why didn't I start off talking to the kids? It seemed like a setup and it was. Stew knows I can never disappoint my kids unless it's an emergency. But I thought to myself that this was an emergency.

Nicole and Doug told me to sit down. Doug handed me a Dr. Seuss book called *Oh, The Places You'll Go!* It talks about the ups and downs of life—in poetry of course, and at a level for a child to understand.

I was completely taken aback. All the years I had read Dr. Seuss to my kids and now they had me reading it to me! "Read it out loud," Doug said, "and think about what it's telling you."

The book described the wonders of life—the "great sights," the "high heights" that are possible. Then the scene shifted to the opposite—the downside, the disappointments that happen to even the best of us:

> *Wherever you go,*
> *you'll top all the rest.*
> *Except when you don't.*
> *Because sometimes you won't.*

Then Nicole started to speak. "Mom, this election isn't about you. There's no way you can drop out. What will that tell the world about women? That we can't take the heat? That we let the polls and the press push us out?

Exhausted but exhilarated, here I am with Anita Hill and Barbra Streisand after my election in 1992 as Senator from California.

Stewart and me at our engagement dinner in 1960. He was 21; I was 19.

Me and the kids in 1968. Nicole (my co-author) is on the left and Doug (now a lawyer!) is on the right.

courtesy Tom Gibbons

Stewart and me at a relaxed moment at the home of Dianne Feinstein.

Congressman Frank McCloskey of Indiana and me at our first Presidential reception, at the White House in 1983.

In 1983, Congresswoman Gerry Ferraro and I became good friends in the House of Representatives.

photo: Sharon Christovich

My mom, Sophie Levy, and I receive news of my first Congressional victory in 1983. She was my best supporter, making xerox copies of every article that mentioned me for all my relatives. Very sadly for me, she died before I was elected to the Senate.

Congresswomen Barbara Mikulski and Barbara Boxer at the home of our mutual supporter Duane Guarett of California in 1984, during Mikulski's Senatorial race.

At a ceremony honoring women in unusual professions, in 1984.

This is the spare part that cost $850—and got me into military procurement reform.

Singing our way into the gym in 1985. Special guest at the gym dinner—then-Vice President George Bush (far right). From left to right: Congressman Ed Boland, who headed the gym committee, and Congresswomen Pat Schroeder, Marilyn Lloyd, Barbara Mikulski, Lindy Boggs, Mary Rose Okar, and Marcy Kaptur. That's me between Pat and Marilyn.

Campaigning for reelection to my House seat in 1985. I always visit child care centers and children—they remind me of why I'm in public life.

Pat Schroeder and me discussing strategy on the House steps in approximately 1985. Pat, the dean of the women of the House, has served since 1973.

In 1989, I organized a pro-choice contingent of members of Congress to march together at a rally in Washington, D.C.

At the pro-choice rally. Left to right: Rep. George Miller, me, Rep. Howard Wolfe, Sen. Barbara Mikulski, Rep. Nancy Pelosi, Rep. Tom Downey, Rep. Claudine Schneiller.

courtesy Jo Fielder

Campaigning with Texas governor Ann Richards in 1992 at a hugely successful EMILY's fundraiser in San Francisco.

Barry E. Levine, Inc.

Fabulous songwriters Alan and Marilyn Bergman, who introduced me to everyone they knew in Los Angeles.

Supporting a woman's right to choose at a pro-choice rally in San Francisco in 1992.

courtesy Jo Fielder

The kids and me right after their mom became a Senator, November, 1993.

official White House photo

Stew, me and our son Doug talking to the First Lady after she addressed the Democratic Senators on the health care issue.

The women of the Senate in early 1993 after a discussion with First Lady Hillary Rodham Clinton. Left to right: Carol Moseley-Braun, Patty Murray, Barbara Mikulski, me, Dianne Feinstein, Nancy Kassebaum.

In 1993, soon after I was sworn in, I co-chaired a dinner for the Democratic Senatorial Campaign Committee. Here's the Vice President with me. Looking on: Senate Majority Leader George Mitchell, House Speaker Tom Foley, House Majority Leader Richard Gephardt.

Senator Paul Simon, the President and me discussing the budget in early 1993.

Seven Congresswomen walk over to the Senate to ask for a hearing on Anita Hill's charges. I had never seen us so determined.

Nicole told me that I would win because people would understand that I was fighting for them and their kids—but that I had to start by fighting for myself. Doug nodded in agreement. "It's only 90 days 'til the primary," he said. "Just give it all you have and see what happens. You can't quit."

I was stunned as all of this was happening, but I soon knew that I had absolutely no choice but to continue the insanity of running for statewide office in California. The "60 Minutes" show about EMILY's List gave credence to everything Nicole said. Women were counting on me to be tough, and my toughness would give them strength. And their battles—single mothers raising kids without child support, working women barely getting by, gutsy survivors of breast cancer and abusive relationships—made mine seem like a birthday party. And their problems would last much longer than 90 days. But you can't fight for the people if you can't fight for yourself—for your self-respect and dignity. No one ever thought that I could win at this point, so I figured I might as well do my best and come as close as I could.

There was a lot of hugging that night. Stew was still watching the game. When he came downstairs I told him the kids had kept me in the race. He'd known that would happen; he had planned it with them. My husband doesn't waste words. He just smiled and said, "It's only three more months."

The Race Heats Up

Stew started to travel with me more. Having him on the trail with me kept me more normal and grounded. He was usually pretty calm, but there were times when it got to him. One day he said he had to get away, so he went to the movies to see a double feature. Unfortunately for him, the second feature was "Bob Roberts," a movie about a Senate candidate. "I can't get away from it no matter what I do," he said. Then he saw a trailer for "Dracula" and said he thought of my opponent. He was nervous, even though he wouldn't admit it.

Of course, the 30-second negative television spots about me were broadcast all over California. We had fallen asleep with the TV on after one tough day when I sat upright in bed with a jolt: I had just heard one or another of my opponents blasting me with, "Barbara Boxer's a no good, miserable, incompetent nitwit," or something close to that. "God, they're even in my dreams!" I told Stew.

On to November

It turned out that my kids were right—and I won the primary, defeating two major opponents by a healthy margin. I was the party's nominee! (Some outer applause to go with the inner applause.) For a while, things went along well, although the pace was grueling and I began to wonder just how much more I could endure. But exhausting as the race was, it was exhilarating, too. As we covered the state from north to south and back again, from San Diego to Los Angeles, from Fresno to Mendocino, from San Francisco to Santa Barbara, I met thousands of people who were as excited as I was about changing the direction of the country.

Though the campaign had ugly moments, it had beautiful ones as well, and those kept me going: the people who sent in modest contributions with a note saying how much they believed in me; the thousands who bought my yellow and black "boxer shorts" at house parties all over the state; the volunteers in the office who gave so generously of their time hour after endless hour; the school children who wanted to hold my hand; the nurses who became a statewide network of supporters because they knew how much health care reform needs a leader; the premature babies in hospitals, who are there because their mothers never had pre-natal care, whom I held for as long as the nurses let me; the elderly in nursing homes who never wanted me to leave; people with HIV or AIDS waiting for the cure and counting on me to fight for them; the kids in public schools, too many of whom had to share and ration paper and pencils; families living around toxic dumps who needed an advocate; the fishermen who feared losing their professions because of a lack of water policy; the small-business owners faced with a credit crunch and a recession at the same time; the defense workers who needed a real conversion plan, not just talk; the family planning workers scared of clinic violence; the youngsters who wanted so much to go to college but feared the financial squeeze; the thousands and thousands of women of every age and race whose faces blend into beautiful, hopeful images.

All of them placed so much trust in me—Barbara Boxer, a very average, very human person. I think that's what they liked—that I'm average. If I can do it, they can do it. I must do it, I thought every night as I fell into bed, feet aching, voice hoarse, mind numb. Then the alarm rang at about 6:30 a.m.—"Oh! The Places You'll Go!"

Down to the Wire

I had hoped for a campaign on the issues, a genuine debate of differing points of view, offering clear choices to the voters. It was not to be. My Republican opponent decided to use his commercials not to lay out his ideas but to attack me. This wasn't too shocking in itself—after all, I did hold a substantial lead after Labor Day, two months before Election Day—and I'd learned to expect to take some knocks. But I was surprised by his decision to go with an almost exclusively negative "buy" for his spots. Since I'd been holding the lead, the Democratic Senatorial Campaign Committee didn't view my race with alarm, and sent their dollars to other races, while my opponent received large contributions from the Republican Senatorial Campaign. This meant that he could do early TV—he could start taking out ads two months before the election.

My opponent's campaign advisers reasoned that since many voters didn't know me, they would use the TV ads to paint a picture of Barbara Boxer before I could. Needless to say, that picture was of a selfish, out-of-touch politician, totally unrecognizable to anyone who knew me. But they were aiming at the millions who didn't. Remember, California is a nation-sized state with a population of 31 million, and I had never run for statewide office before.

The negative spots worked. I began to drop in the polls. My staff knew it before the press did, and when the press found out, they had a field day. My colleague Dianne Feinstein was way out in front, and there I was, starting to lose my race. The skeptical columns started to appear: Two women can't do it. She's too liberal. She's too this. She's too that.

Running Against the Polls

Our problem was that we couldn't afford to go on TV until two and a half to three weeks before Election Day, while the opposition's ads had been on for weeks and weeks. We'd planned great television spots, but we knew that once we went on TV, we had to saturate the market to win, and we just couldn't afford to go on early. (It cost $25,000 for one well-placed 30-second TV spot.)

Even the calmest of my supporters were turning into nervous wrecks. Soon the phones began to ring, with advice from my backers. "Go on TV now," they begged, "even a little will help!" In some of the most touching moments of the race, perfect strangers lined up at my Los Angeles office and made campaign contributions of one and two dollars. "You *have* to win," they'd say. "But go on TV now!"

I give much credit to my campaign team—Joel Bradshaw, Karen Olick, Rose Kapolczynski, Jim Margolis—for sticking to our game plan. We had to wait it out until we knew we could saturate the airwaves and not squander our media dollars in little small TV buys which would have no impact. I trusted them completely because they made sense but my resolve was tested every hour after each loving and nervous supporter challenged the strategy.

Now we had another big decision to make. If I had been as damaged by my opponent's negative campaign as we thought, did we have a chance to win by staging completely positive TV spots? We decided to stick to the issues and tell Californians where my opponent stood on them—that he thought *Roe v. Wade* was a "crazy" decision; that he thought everyone had the right to carry an Uzi; that he wanted to drill oil off California's magnificent coast. We hit the voters' TV screens, with about two and a half weeks to go until Election Day. By that time, we knew we were tied in the polls. Every night we tested those waters and ever so slowly, we began to pull away—painfully slowly, our lead returned. We were ahead by three to five points. But the press continued to run "tied in the polls" stories even when we knew we were in front.

The Home Stretch

In every tough, difficult election, there comes a time when there is only one thing that keeps you going, and that is the certainty that it will end. With elections, there are no do-overs, no cancelling for foul weather, no reprieves. Unless, God help you, there's a tie, once it's over, it's over.

About the time we started running our TV ads, I started the mental countdown. I fantasized about the peacefulness of my existence after November 3—whatever happened. I visualized the pleasures of reading a novel, going to a jazz concert, inviting people to dinner at the house without charging them! In short, all the joys of leading a normal life.

Then, the weekend before the election, my opponent admitted to the press that he had taken his lady friend to a nude bar. And he blamed my campaign for the story breaking when we had absolutely nothing to do with it! This was a twist I'd never anticipated—I'd staked out the strong turf of pointing out our differences on health care, choice, the environment and jobs. Frankly, I didn't care where my opponent spent his spare time. I cared about what he would do as a United States Senator. But political races take crazy twists and turns.

We continued our polling every night until Election Day—we were ahead but it was close, very close. On Election Eve, Stew and I and our best friends from youth, Gloria and Paul Littman, had traveled to Los Angeles to thank all of our supporters there. Renowned lyricist Marilyn Bergman, an old and dear friend, had promised to introduce me to everyone she knew in Los Angeles, and she did. All they wanted from me was a commitment to fight for a better California. In 24 hours I would know if I would be able to do that from the Senate.

On Election Day, Stew and I went to vote together, as we had done so many times before. That's when the feeling of relief hit. *It was over!* Back at the house, I had invited a few of our close friends over for bagels—comfort food for me—and the big wait. Later we would go over to the Fairmont Hotel for the hoped-for victory party. The wonderful Phil Angelides, chairman of the Democratic Party of California, who had done so much to help my campaign, was getting everything arranged there. My incomparable team—Rose, Karen, Jim, Joel and our pollster Mark Mellman—would be there to pace with me, cry with me or laugh with me.

I will never forget the phone ringing at about noon California time. Someone who knew someone who knew someone at one of the TV stations had heard that I was winning in the exit polls by about five or six points, and they believed that was an accurate reflection of the race. I decided that no matter who this source was, I would believe it. I screamed, and it must have been akin to a primal scream. Everyone ran into the kitchen, and I told them the news. Tears and kisses and smiles were all I saw, and then our friend Paul, in his very calm way, said, "This is not the final word—it's not over yet." I knew I should listen to him, but I was too tired, too relieved. The call *had* to be right. But I did decide to go through the rest of what is always the longest day of your life, with a tiny bit of skepticism—just in case.

The family stopped at Allegro's, a wonderful Italian restaurant in North Beach, where we met friends and supporters, among them my former boss John Burton and his daughter Kimi, who had heard about the exit polls and were ecstatic. We also saw Dianne Feinstein, who was trying to contain her excitement, too. Her exit poll numbers were exquisite.

The rest of the evening is a blur of a blur, but the photos tell the story. At two a.m., my opponent conceded in a telephone call, and then I really believed it had happened. I ended up staying up until about four a.m. with friends Marilyn Bergman, Gloria Littman, and Shelley List. We were starving and sent for room service at about two a.m., but it never appeared, although the hotel kept saying they had sent it. (And they did!—to Dianne Feinstein's suite, where her happy but weary warriors were all too glad for the mistake.)

I left the next day for four days of R & R, then took the red-eye to Washington, D.C. for orientation regarding Senate procedures and committee assignments.

Strangers No More

On January 4 the swearing-in took place. As I walked down the aisle of the Senate, escorted by my colleague, Senator Dianne Feinstein, and as I looked around that beautiful chamber at the bright, colorful suits of the newly elected women, all of which cried out, "It's different now," I thought of my mother and father and all the challenges they faced as new Americans. My only unfulfilled wish of that day was that they could have been there with me.

In May 1993, 14 months to the day that I decided to drop out of the race for Senate, but didn't because of my kids, Majority Leader George Mitchell gave the following speech to all the Senators and their spouses. Stew and I listened as he said:

> Last year at this dinner, I addressed you as Senators and their wives. This year we're all pleased to be joined by new women Senators and their spouses. It's a positive change, for women and for the nation.

The presence of five new women in the Senate is a visible and public repudiation of the view that women should be barred from certain occupations and opportunities. That restrictive view of the role of women has a long history throughout the world, even here in the United States.

One hundred and twenty years ago, the Supreme Court denied a lawyer from Illinois the right to practice her profession because she was a woman. The Court said: "The natural and proper timidity and delicacy which belongs to the female sex evidently unfits it for many of the occupations of civil life. . . ."

It's obvious that the man who wrote these words—Justice Joseph Bradley—never met Barbara Mikulski or Barbara Boxer. As I said, the case involved the State of Illinois. I wonder what Justice Bradley would think if he were here tonight and looked out at the Senator from Illinois, Carol Moseley-Braun? At the very least, he'd marvel at the change she represents.

This change has been achieved for the most part by women themselves—slowly, very slowly, over intense opposition, in the face of much ridicule.

Listen to these words:

"The world taught women nothing skillful and then said her work was valueless. It permitted her no opinions and [then] said she did not know how to think. It forbade her to speak in public and [then] said [she] had no orators. It denied her the schools and [then] said [she] had no genius. It robbed her of every vestige of responsibility and then called her weak." Those were the words of Carrie Chapman Catt, speaking to a women's suffrage convention in 1902, 91 years ago.

Change in America may be unending, but it is not always swift. Tonight we honor change in the Senate. It's a welcome change. Our new Senators will be a force for a better Senate and a better America.

Toward Tomorrow

When the suffragettes got the vote for women in 1919, they thought that women would vote in their own self-interest. That did not happen. At first, not too many women voted. Then when they did they handed over their ballots to their husbands or their fathers or their brothers or their priests or their rabbis or their ministers.

We are now in a new revolution of women in America. The "miracle" of 1992 reflected not only the fact that women tripled their numbers in the United States Senate, but that the women of America realized that they were missing from political life. They got involved and they worked hard and they convinced others to do the same. They convinced their husbands and brothers and sons that they needed their support. Thus the "miracle" of 1992—not a miracle unearned, but surely a miracle a long time in coming.

Will there be more? Only you can answer that question.

PART III

PRESENT CHALLENGES

Chapter Eight

The Domestic Agenda, Stupid!

There were six major female candidates in the November, 1992 races for the United States Senate who were non-incumbents. They were all over the country—from California to Pennsylvania, from Illinois to Missouri to Washington State. Except for the two women from California, Dianne Feinstein and myself, none of the other candidates knew each other. And even Dianne and I never checked on issues with one another. We had taken different stands on issues several times over the years, and certainly had always presented our stands differently.

But something happened in the election of 1992.

Presidential candidate Bill Clinton reportedly had a sign on his wall that read, "The Economy, Stupid!" to remind him what he wanted to stress in his basic speeches, writings, and media advertisements. And we women candidates all had an unwritten sign in our heads that read: "The Domestic Agenda!"

We women were all committed to putting forward an agenda for our states and for America that shifted the focus away from the military and foreign policy to our families, to our children, to our health care system, to our jobs, to our economy—the "domestic agenda."

Critics called us isolationists; in fact, one of my opponents in the primary called me a "trendy isolationist" whose views would lead to an unstable and unpredictable world. I find that charge absolutely absurd.

The truth is that unless America's strength comes from within we will fail as the model of democracy and a free market economy and the world will indeed become more unstable and unpredictable. Further, we will be unable to assist emerging democracies in the ways we would like. It costs dollars to be one of the leaders on the world stage.

For us to be strong from within we need to ensure that our people have hope for themselves and even more hope for their children.

Strong from Within

We must always remember that it is the power of democracy and economic freedom that leads the world in our direction. The former Soviet Union, too, had massive military might, but the Soviet Union oppressed its people with an economic and political system that trapped them in hopelessness. Ultimately, military power was not the determining factor in winning over hearts and minds as was evident as artists and writers and average people hungry for freedom tore down the walls of oppression. (Nor has this been the case only in Eastern Europe. In the Philippines under Ferdinand Marcos the Philippine people stood up against tanks and guns in order to get democracy and a share of economic justice.)

Now, in order to make sure we never go back to the terrible days of the Cold War, we must make certain that economic and social justice and a decent life for our people is synonymous with the word America.

No one should believe that the American dream—a good job, a decent place to live, a good education for their children—is guaranteed to everyone. But every American should know that a fair *chance* at the American dream is guaranteed by our society. It sure was to me and to the other women who were on the Senate campaign trail in 1992.

The Cold War didn't end a moment too soon. The Soviet Union went broke not only because of a bankrupt ideology, but because the arms race led the country into bankruptcy.

When American businesses go bankrupt, they file Chapter 11, are given a chance to regroup and pay off their debts, and hopefully, start again. Chapter 11 for the Soviet Union meant its demise. Its wealth had been eaten up by weapons systems and KGB agents and the drain of maintaining a military presence throughout the world. The government controlled everything, with the main priority being an equalizing of the military power with the West. Their people suffered the economic and political consequences of having no hope and no freedom.

To me, the real proof of failure had long been demonstrated by the number of Soviet citizens who wished to leave. For years, I had worked with colleagues to free Soviet Jews and other political prisoners. When I considered the religious and political persecution and hatreds there, I couldn't understand why the authorities fought so hard to stop people whom they detested from leaving. Then I realized that had these groups gotten out, the numbers of people wanting to leave would rise to levels intolerable to the Soviet authorities. Consequently, I learned the vast majority of Soviet citizens didn't have a prayer of leaving the Soviet Union. Jews and other "religious minorities" had at least a chance because they were considered outsiders with "homelands" of their own to which they could go.

No, I was never an isolationist, trendy or otherwise; I just knew that those yearning for freedom were counting on the greatest of all democratic experiments to be a roaring success—and a model for them.

Presidential candidate Bill Clinton understood this when he defined our strength not only in terms of our military but our economic strength.

In President Clinton's acceptance speech at the Democratic National Convention, he said, "We meet at a special moment in history, you and I. The Cold War is over. Soviet Communism has collapsed, and our values— freedom, democracy, individual rights, free enterprise— they have triumphed around the world. And yet just as we have won the Cold War abroad, we are losing the battles for economic opportunity and social justice here at home."

He recalled his very personal experience:

> I never met my father. He was killed in a car wreck on a rainy road three months before I was born, driving from Chicago to Arkansas to see my mother.
>
> After that, my mother had to support us, so we lived with my grandparents while she went back to Louisiana to study nursing. I can still see her clearly tonight through the eyes of a three-year-old, kneeling at the railroad station and weeping as she put me back on the train to Arkansas with my grandmother.
>
> She endured that pain because she knew her sacrifice was the only way she could support me and give me a better life. My mother taught me. She taught me about family and hard work and sacrifice. She held steady through tragedy after tragedy, and

she held our family—my brother and I—together through tough times.

As a child, I watched her go off to work each day at a time when it wasn't always easy to be a working mother. As an adult. I watched her fight off breast cancer, and again she has taught me a lesson in courage. And always, always, always she taught me to fight.

That's why I'll fight to create high paying jobs so that parents can afford to raise their children today. That's why I'm so committed to make sure every American gets the health care that saved my mother's life and that women's health care gets the same attention as men's. That's why I'll fight to make sure women in this country receive respect and dignity, whether they work in the home, out of the home or both.

Of course we must never underestimate the dangers in the world and our military budget must be threat-based so that we can meet any threat; in addition, we must be a leader in the community of nations, forging international agreements to respond to trouble spots and foster world peace, with a priority of stopping nuclear proliferation.

Investing for National Success

President Clinton has surrounded himself with those who understand the world challenges we face but the Clinton teams, both those in foreign policy and in domestic policy, understand that the end of the Cold War meant the beginning of the "Economic War" and that for us to be in competition means some new weapons and new troops. Those troops include the entrepreneurs and the workers, wise elected leaders, an informed electorate, and teachers to nurture and encourage. The weapons also include great schools and universities, technology and patient capital.

President Clinton's "investment" strategy is crucial to our success in the Economic War. We are falling far behind our allies in many categories of government investment.

His plan to promote private investment is crucial as well.

Focusing on the domestic agenda means that our people will be more productive. If a worker no longer has to worry about adequate child care, productivity will rise; if moms and dads know there is a fair family leave policy after the birth or adoption of a child, productivity will rise; if workers know they won't lose their health care by moving to another job that they really want, productivity will rise; if young people can go to college because they get decent college loans, America will be more competitive, because as Labor Secretary Robert Reich has said, the best jobs will go to the best educated.

We know that certain nations—Japan and Germany certainly leap to mind—have invested far more in civilian research and development than America has. During the 1980s, 80 percent of America's governmental investment in research and development went into the military. When these investments shift we will begin coming up with civilian technologies, such as environmental clean-up technology and super computers, that other nations will clamor for.

The Domestic Agenda and the 1992 Campaign

The domestic agenda! Independent of one another, that's what the women candidates spoke about on the campaign trail. All of the Democratic women Senate nominees touched on the same theme when speaking at the Democratic National Convention, in July of 1992.

They took to the floor of the Convention amid huge cheers.

Carol Moseley-Braun began:

> Our cities can be rebuilt, our economy reconstructed, our environment saved, and health care provided for every American when we remember that the people who serve in high public office are the servants, and not the masters, of the people who elect them. We can ensure that women have the freedom as equal citizens under the law to make reproductive choices. And we can rekindle the hope that the American dream is not some old fashioned fantasy, but a living reality. We can change the world.
>
> As St. Augustine wrote, "Hope has two lovely daughters, Anger and Courage—anger at the way things are, and the courage to change them." Tonight as I look out over this room of warriors in the good fight ahead, let me assure you that your anger at the way things are will fuel a courageous fight for change. This is the Democratic mandate. This is the message we will take to the American people.

I was next:

> All Americans share a great and glorious dream. But tonight, many of us again are worried about our children's future, because the American dream of economic security is slipping away from us. Our challenge tonight is one that every American understands. It is to bring back the dream—bring back the dream. And together with Bill Clinton and Al Gore, we will meet that challenge. We will.

When America's schools are ranked 21st in he world, how can we ever produce the best and the brightest? When the cost of a child's education—a college education—or a grandmother's medical needs have gone out of control, how can the generation in the middle make ends meet?

We have to bring the money home and invest it in our children, in health research, in our environment, and create hundreds of thousands of jobs. It is time to take care of our own.

And we must never let government get in the middle of our most private decisions. I will fight for a woman's right to choose.

I grew up believing that the United States Senate was a place where the American dream was protected and enhanced. And I truly believe that the women who are running for the United States Senate will carry that dream with them—and we will crack open the doors of the United States Senate. We will open them wide and start running a country, not a country club.

Jean Lloyd Jones of Iowa followed me:

I am a mother and I am a grandmother, and I want to leave a legacy to the next generation—a legacy of clean water and clean air, not a planet fouled with industrial waste and poisoned by toxic chemicals.

I want a national budget that promotes peace, star schools and not "Star Wars," a nation that cares for its sick and elderly and not a nation that tries to balance its budget by trading arms to all the world's dictators. I want a government that can't be bought, a government that guarantees the rights of equal opportunity to all its citizens, and a Supreme Court that will uphold a woman's right to choose.

Next was Lynn Yeakel of Pennsylvania:

> I was a college sophomore when John F. Kennedy was nominated for the Democratic Presidential nomination 32 years ago tonight. When John Kennedy called upon all of us to look not at what was but to shape what will be, that was a message that profoundly affected my life.
>
> Come dream what I dream. I dream of an America where there is a sensible balance between national security and family security. I dream of an America where no worker is denied a job, no child goes hungry or homeless, no person is uneducated, and no one goes without health care.

Closing this segment was Dianne Feinstein:

> 1992 isn't just the Year of the Woman; it's the year of the people, because this year people—men and women working together—are going to take back our government—and take back the White House from George Bush.
>
> Our opponents deride this wave of change as "gender politics," but they just still don't get it. It's not about gender; it's about an agenda—an agenda of change: an economic plan to grow our economy, to create jobs, to protect our quality of life and to protect a woman's right to choose.
>
> Today, America's greatest national security threat is her domestic home front, and the battles are education; health care, including AIDS and breast cancer; jobs; infrastructure; the budget deficit; and

the environment. It's time we had a team led by Bill Clinton and Al Gore, who will wage and win that war.

And in speech after speech, in state after state, we expanded on these issues to define the domestic agenda.

Health Care

One of the major issues on the domestic agenda has to be health care. It's an issue that touches us all.

There was lots of discussion when First Lady Hillary Rodham Clinton was selected by the President to head the Health Care Reform Task Force.

I thought it was a brilliant stroke! Mrs. Clinton's analytical and organizational skills—plus her perspective as a woman—make her a natural for the position.

It isn't always the case, of course, but I think most doctor appointments for children are made by women; most of those sitting up with sick kids or parents are women; women understand perhaps with more poignancy the nightmare of an unwanted pregnancy or the inability to become pregnant; they are more of the nurses and nurses aides who see most directly the agony of nursing homes and the expensive failures that exist in a system where 100,000 Americans per month lose their health insurance. Is this female experience needed around the table when health care decisions are made? Absolutely.

I believe that the ongoing fight for health care will be very much on the agenda of the women in the Senate as well as in the House of Representatives, and Mrs. Clinton's voice on this subject is a prelude of the female voices that will follow.

Spending Priorities

The domestic agenda! It was no coincidence that the Democratic women of the U.S. Senate, class of '92, were heard day after day in the fight for President Clinton's jobs stimulus bill. Our focus is the domestic agenda and jobs are high on the list. Senator Robert Byrd of West Virginia recognized the efforts of the women and thanked us for our strength during the long and tedious filibuster led by the Republicans who stopped the jobs bill of March, 1993 from coming to a vote.

I thought Patty Murray said it best. "For years, Americans have been paying and getting little in return: waste, abuse, and the rich getting richer. People in this country are desperate. Look at the state of the American family, and then tell a poor mother that WIC is not an emergency," she said. "Tell a person who is living with AIDS that Ryan White funding is not an emergency. Tell a child trying to learn that Head Start funding is not an emergency. Tell a child whose parents cannot afford it that immunization is not an emergency. Tell our nation's 1.8 million jobless that unemployment benefits are not an emergency." She went on to say,"It's easy to forget about the little guy, Mr. President, but I cannot."

It was especially nice for Senator Murray, as a Senate newcomer, when Senator Byrd, on the Senate floor, said, "Mr. President . . . I have listened to the speech by the distinguished junior Senator of Washington. She has made a speech that is succinct, cogent, and persuasive, and it contains common sense. She spoke with poise, with confidence, and with high dedication to purpose. She is having an impact on this Senate and I, again, congratulate her."

Senator Wendell Ford of Kentucky was the next to speak that day. He said, "Let me just say to my colleague from

Washington, I was watching her on the television and had to come to the floor to really see and get a better feel. She talked about little people but gave a tall speech."

Cutting Government Waste

Setting priorities for spending is crucial, but we will also be stronger when we stop wasting money in government. I know that there are those who exaggerate, saying that we can completely cure the deficit just by cutting out waste, and I'm not suggesting that, but I do know that there is waste across government and it lies in overhead, in procurement and in misplaced priorities.

I know about waste in the military first-hand, thanks to a constituent who walked into my Congressional office in 1983 when I was a new member of the House of Representatives. A small-businessman, he showed me a little four-inch spare part that looked like a tiny bracket. He asked me what I thought it cost. I held the bracket in my hand and asked what its military function was. He said it had no military function at all; that it just went on the wall of a C-5A cargo plane and had wire wrapped around it.

"Twenty-five bucks," I said, upping my estimate since I could tell he was leading me in the direction of an over-priced part.

"Wrong," he gloated. "It's costing taxpayers 850 dollars."

From there our discussion turned into a sketch worthy of "Saturday Night Live."

"No," I said. "Yes," he answered. I was incredulous. Later that day I called in my trusted aide, Claudette Josephson, who had come with me from California to get the office going. I asked her to guess what the part cost. She held it in her hand as I told her the price. Her reaction was basically the same as mine—except that she was so mad she threw the part across the office. We both called in Sam Chapman, who was and still is my chief of staff, and he agreed that we had to act. Even though I was just a freshman member of Congress, I knew no one else was doing anything about publicizing this scandal. I also knew that if you want to be effective on an issue, you have to take it to the people. So I did.

This was 1983, when the military could do no wrong. Billions of dollars were being pumped into the Pentagon with nary a care. Questioning the military industrial complex in 1983 bordered on the unpatriotic. Well, I thought that blowing the whistle on waste, fraud and abuse was quite patriotic, so I carried on.

I remember debating the Pentagon on a late-night TV talk show. I was scolded and lectured. "What do you know?" they asked. "You just came up with one example of a problem that was not system-wide . . . it was an 'isolated example.' " I heard those words over and over again. I said that it didn't take a doctoral degree to figure out when you're getting ripped off, especially when a business person calls it to your attention and says that he can make that part for $825 less than what the Pentagon is paying. I was determined to find more examples and spoke to my colleague from Iowa, Berkeley Bedell. He was approaching the issue from another side—the need to involve small businesses in the production of spare parts for the military. He was right on target.

What was happening back then was that the prime defense contractors were producing these spare parts. They had no experience in making brackets or toilet seat covers or coffee pots or ladders or hammers or wrenches, and when they produced them they added all their major overhead into their costs. The Pentagon was also causing problems by designing these items like Cadillacs. For example, the coffee pots for cargo planes that were discovered by the Project for Military Procurement's terrific staff aides Dina Raisor and Donna Martin and my own irrepressible staffer-turned-San Francisco radio talk show host, Bernie Ward, wound up costing $7,500. How could this be? Because it was designed to withstand such large gravity forces that I think it would have still been perking if the plane crashed. Talk about over-engineering!

Bedell and I teamed up and got legislation passed that forced competition in the spare parts area, and happily, the Small Business Administration has reported that this legislation has saved taxpayers over one billion dollars so far. But we must do more of this kind of procurement because these are the "cuts that are painless"—and because defense contractors are taking advantage of their country.

What happened to JFK's "Ask not what your country can do for you; rather ask what you can do for your country"? Was it replaced by "Ask how you can rip off my country today"? That's what some of these contractors were doing as a way of life, and unfortunately, it goes on to this day. I think our bill—coupled with some disciplinary action—really sent a strong message to defense contractors. But now we are seeing this kind of thing turn up in the Environmental Protection Agency's Superfund program.

Fortunately Senator Frank Lautenberg of New Jersey is on top of it and acting to put an end to "unallowable" costs such as fancy dinners and ballooning expense accounts. The women in the Senate will be real fighters here, working with our colleagues. We've all managed households, and we clearly understand that there isn't one dime to waste—anywhere.

The entire government procurement system needs to be examined and revised. When I served on the House Armed Services Committee I learned that there are about

250,000 procurement officers—that's the same population as the county in which I live. That's half the population of some states. Imagine how much we could save if all the branches of the military combined procurement—and how much better it would be if there were a civilian procurement corps so we could stop the revolving door of procurement officers retiring from the military and going to work for the very companies they just supervised! (The revolving door in the military was a passion of now-retired Congressman Charles Bennett of Florida. This decent man spent many years trying to stop it. I teamed up with him and we did make some progress but we need to do more.) In their "re-inventing government" plans, the Clinton Administration is on the right track. There is much to be saved!

The Environment

As I will explore in the following chapters, women will be voices for children and for choice, and I believe they will also be a voice for a clean and healthful environment. There will be those who will try to pose a false choice—that to have a clean and healthy environment we have to destroy our economy. That theory is way off the mark. As a matter of fact, there can be no economic growth without a sound environmental policy. I am pleased that Vice President Al Gore carries that message every day. His voice is missed in the Senate, but I believe that the women there will swell the chorus for protection of the environment.

As I said in a speech before the Planning and Conservation League last year, the myth of a conflict between a prospering economy and a clean environment is one that was handed down from Ronald Reagan to his Interior Secretary James Watt and then to two of George Bush's foot soldiers, Chief of Staff John Sununu and Vice President Dan Quayle.

It's easy to disprove that myth: just look at Eastern Europe. When the wall came down, we could hardly see those legendary cities through all the soot and smog and filth. It is hard to tell which is the most rotten—the air, the soil, the water, or the economy of Eastern Europe. They will need our help on all fronts.

The Bush-Quayle Administration was devoid of original ideas for jump-starting the U.S. economy, so it quickly disavowed the promise of an environmental Presidency and invoked the myth. And it placed in its sights the very resources we should be protecting: our wetlands and forests, our coasts and the Arctic National Wildlife Refuge, our energy savings programs and our endangered species.

It is clear to me that if we cut all our forests down, there will be none left to manage and work, and few pharmaceutical products for us to discover; if we destroy our ocean and coast with off-shore drilling, we ruin two very big industries in America—tourism and fishing; if we're trapped every day in a traffic nightmare, we can't be productive; if we don't clean up the hazards in our soil, it will be sterile; if we waste precious water, our cities, suburbs, farms and public lands will all suffer. And obviously, if we can't breathe, we can't work.

We should pursue clean energy sources while lessening our reliance on imported energy by conservation. At present, half of our balance of trade deficit comes from importing oil—a tremendous percentage. There's no way we should have to be so dependent. Energy conservation creates jobs, and development of safe alternatives will lessen the risk of a Chernobyl-style nuclear disaster here. (Talk about something that is bad for the economy—a nuclear accident on that scale can cost a lot more than dollars.) Encouraging people to take steps like weatherization will create jobs as well as save energy—an estimated 6,000 jobs for every 100 million dollars spent on home weatherization. We should pursue greater fuel efficiency in automobiles as well.

Defense Priorities

I predict that the Democratic women of the Senate will also work for a better distribution of costs surrounding our military obligations, as we focus on a domestic agenda. Retired Admiral Eugene Carroll of the Center for Defence Information reports that now, after the end of the Cold War, America is still spending over $100 billion defending our allies in Europe and Asia. Clearly, we need to better distribute the burden.

We know today's world is very unstable and that America has a big stake in bringing about stability and promoting new ways of handling regional conflicts. That's why it is time for truly cooperative security agreements with the countries of the world who understand that there must be some clear and straightforward rules that respect internationally recognized borders and civilized behavior. John D. Steinbruner, the co-author of "A New Concept of Cooperative Security," a paper published by the Brookings Institution, laid it out very well for me. Steinbruner says: "If the period of the Cold War can be summarized as a competition in military development, the emerging new era can be projected as a search for reliable control over the results of that competition." That means building on agreements to dismantle nuclear weapons and controlling proliferation of conventional and nuclear weapons. It also means more cooperation between the ground forces of different nations, and coordination of intelligence functions—and it should mean everyone doing their fair share.

This doesn't mean that we give up the right to act in our own best interest, but there is no question that ours is a changing world, and where the Soviet threat resulted in our placing long-range nuclear missiles aimed at fixed targets in the Warsaw Pact, the new challenges will likely be incidents that will require highly mobile forces. Today we need to have a threat-based military, not one based on a Cold War policy. I had an opportunity to question the representatives of the Central Intelligence Agency at an open meeting of the Joint Economic Committee on June 1, 1993. I asked if they believed that it would be possible to face a united force of nations arrayed against America. They gave me a clear-cut no. I was surprised at how direct they were. Intelligence professionals agree: today the threat is different.

Cooperative agreements and streamlining of procurement should be pursued so that military spending can safely be reduced to bring about real deficit reduction. And as we downsize our military we must invest in dual-use technologies so that those on the defense side of business can convert their technologies to civilian products—something that is already beginning to happen with some new government grants and matched by private dollars from resourceful entrepreneurs. In addition, worker retraining is a Clinton Administration priority so that we don't lose the skills and expertise of those defense workers.

An Agenda for Public Safety

The domestic agenda is the women's agenda.

I believe women in the Senate will work hard to stop gun violence.

After the brutal attack at an office in San Francisco in July, 1993 by a deranged gunman who sought revenge for his financial troubles, I checked on gun control bills pending in the Senate.

The bill that deals with the ban on semi-automatic weapons was written by Senator Howard Metzenbaum of Ohio. Essentially, the Metzenbaum bill would ban certain guns, listed by name, and allow the Bureau of Alcohol, Tobacco and Firearms to add all copycat weapons to the list. This last provision is crucially important. The gun used by the San Francisco killer was legal in California—but it should not have been. According to gun experts, the maker of the Intratec TEC-9 (banned in California) basically changed the name of the gun to the TEC-*DC*-9 to get around the law. The Metzenbaum bill is very important.

Most interesting to me was the fact that when I checked on the gun bills, I found that every single Democratic female Senator is on record as backing the Metzenbaum bill—all five of us.

I feel especially strong about gun control because the San Francisco law firm shooting touched the lives of my family, particularly the life of my son Doug, who went to law school with John Scully, one of the victims.

I watched Doug struggle with his loss—trying to seek meaning in it, trying to get over it. He asked me to help him and the family by pushing for viable gun control legislation. I had always supported such legislation but now I will push harder.

I shuddered to learn that in 1990 alone 10,567 Americans were killed by gun violence—there are about that many John Scullys every year in America. And I also began to realize how many thousands of Doug Boxers there are in America—family, friends, acquaintances of victims. So with my family in the gallery on July 13, 1993 I got through the speech that follows. When it was over we cried on each other's shoulders.

Mr. President, it is with tremendous grief and anger that I rise today to speak about the wave of gun violence that has crashed over this nation. Just one week ago today, a massacre erupted at a San Francisco law firm. Shots rang out. People ran for their lives. Eight people lost their lives. When the smoke had cleared, my son lost one of his close friends. John Scully's young life had been cut short, his wife of ten months wounded. John had thrown himself in front of her; he took the bullet she would have taken.

On that tragic day something came between John and his ability to fulfill the promises of a young man bursting with life and love. Something came between him and the ability to be a husband to the woman he had just married in September, to the woman, Michelle, who he gave his life to save. And, something came between him and his ability to continue to be a son and a brother . . . and someday possibly a father and a grandfather. What ended his life? It wasn't a disease. It wasn't an accident. It was a semi-automatic assault weapon set loose in the hands of a deranged gunman.

Gun violence touches too many of our lives. Its victims are our sons and daughters, and neighbors and friends. The sadness runs deep. It's sapping our strength.

Mr. President, this was not California's first gun massacre. How many of us can forget the gunman who opened fire on a Stockton school yard in 1989? Five children were killed. Thirty were wounded. The weapon? It was a semi-automatic assault rifle called an AK-47. The gunman? He had a history of criminal arrests and convictions.

We need to ask ourselves: How can we allow deranged criminals to purchase military-style assault weapons? In 1990, almost 3,000 children and teenagers were murdered with guns. We are losing our children. Between 1984 and 1990, firearms murders of children under 19 increased by 125 percent! We need to ask ourselves: How many more children must die, how many more lives destroyed before we act?

Mr. President, workplace violence is growing. It represents almost 20 percent of all workplace deaths.

Time and time again we hear the gun lobby defending the assault weapons, defending the Uzis. These guns don't kill, they say. Only people kill. (As comedian Will Durst says, poking fun at the gun lobby, "Guns don't kill people, people kill people. Yeah, but it's the bullets that make those little holes that the blood pours out from!") Well, all the well-paid lobbyists and influence peddlers in the world don't change the fact that guns help people kill people. They make it easy to kill people.

These weapons allow criminals to kill from a distance, allow them to kill large numbers of people, and allow them to kill sometimes without knowing or even seeing their victims. It's quick, it's easy, it's impersonal. It's all the things that death . . . in a civilized society . . . should never be.

The NRA tries to tell us that gun control doesn't work, but we need to look at the statistics that the NRA doesn't want us to see. Let's look at the statistics of nations that have gun control laws. In 1990, there were 22 people killed by hand guns in Great Britain; 13 in Sweden, 91 in Switzerland; 87 in Japan; 10 in Australia; and 68 in Canada. But, that very same year, handguns killed 10,567 Americans.

The gun lobby bullies, it distorts, and it mocks. Its ads mock elected officials who have the courage to stand up to them. The gun lobby refuses to accept the fact that most people favor common-sense approaches to decreasing the gun carnage in America. The gun lobby is dangerously out of touch, out of touch with all Americans and even with the very people they claim to represent—the gun owners. Recent surveys have shown that 60 percent of gun owners favor a ban on assault weapons. I ask the gun owners to help us now.

What are we waiting for? Without bans on assault weapons, how many religious zealots like David Koresh are going to be allowed to create their own military stockpiles? Without background checks and waiting periods, how many more criminals are going to leave our gun shops armed to the teeth? Without common-sense laws targeting copycat versions of already-banned assault weapons, how many more gun manufacturers are going to be able to produce the weapon of their choice through this deadly loophole?

We need to pass common-sense gun control laws to curb the sale of assault weapons and take weapons out of the hands of criminals. I want to commend my good friend the distinguished Senator from Ohio, Senator Metzenbaum, for his leadership on this issue. I am proud to be an original co-sponsor of his bill, the Semi-Automatic Assault Weapons Violence Prevention Act of 1993. This bill will give ATF the tools it needs to ban certain classes of semi-automatic assault weapons.

And of course, I want to commend Senator Joe Biden for shepherding the Brady Bill through the Senate.

We need to be clear about the Metzenbaum bill. Assault weapons that serve legitimate sporting purposes would still be legal. But, [the law] would ban guns like the one used in San Francisco, guns designed to do one thing . . . kill a lot of people in a short period of time. Even though an exact replica of it is already banned under California law, the gun used in San Francisco is still perfectly legal. When we pass the Metzenbaum bill, we will direct the ATF to ban these copycat weapons and close this deadly loophole once and for all.

In the memory of John Scully and other innocents who have fallen victim to this continuous slaughter, I ask my colleagues to act quickly to pass gun control legislation. The pain inflicted on family and friends of the victims must be acknowledged not only by comforting words, but also by critical deeds. Let us act with courage and conviction to get these weapons off our streets and out of our communities.

We must not rest until we create an America where children don't go to school armed; an America where gunfire doesn't spray across our communities; and an America where we are appropriately horrified by this violence and are committed to eradicating it. We must not rest until we pass the Brady bill, pass the assault Weapon Act, and stop the violence once and for all.

To John Scully and the others that died at 101 California Street in San Francisco—we must do this in your name.

Senator John Chafee of Rhode Island has introduced a bill to prohibit the manufacture, importation, exportation, sale, purchase, transfer, receipt, possession or transportation of handguns or handgun ammunition; the only exception would be for law enforcement, military guards, or antique collectors and regulated handgun clubs. Senator Chafee calls his bill the "Public Health and Safety Act," and that's an appropriate name.

In a statement given on July 13, 1993, Chafee recalled the San Francisco murders:

> No one in the nation failed to hear of the grisly mass shooting that occurred in the afternoon of July 1 at the offices of San Francisco law firm Petit & Martin in the city's financial district.
>
> Fifty-five-year-old Gian Luigi Ferri, dressed in a dark business suit, entered the building on 101 California Street, made his way to the 34th floor, and began shooting. He shot first into a glass conference room where lawyer Jack Brennan, a graduate of Brown University, and his client, Jody Sposato, sat with defense attorney Sharon O'Roke and court reporter Deanna Eaves, in the process of carrying out a deposition. Brennan and Sposato were killed in that first burst of gunfire; O'Roke and Eaves were seriously wounded. The gunman, armed with three semi-automatic pistols, continued around the perimeter of the office, killing lawyer Allen Berk, and critically wounding Brian Berger. He then took the stairs to the 33rd and 32nd floors, stopping on each and killing or wounding several more employees. Meanwhile, hundreds fled the building, while other panic-stricken employees barricaded themselves in their offices. Emergency crews worked frantically on the dying and wounded and a chaplain with the city fire department administered last rites at the scene for the eight who died.

By the time Ferri took his life in the stairwell on the 30th floor, eight people were dead and six were wounded; the horrible event was the largest mass murder in San Francisco history.

Chafee went to other examples of a gun-violent America.

The incident is horrifying; but in our nation, where there are 70 million handguns in circulation, it is not uncommon. And it certainly is not just lawyers.
Listen to this:

October 1992, Watkins Glen, N.Y.
John Miller walked into the county Department of Social Services in this tiny town, and shot four female employees with a 9-millimeter semi-automatic handgun; all four died instantly. Mr. Miller was angry that he had to pay child support.

January 1993, Miami, Fl.
Steve Alford, a new employee at A & E Aircraft Corporation, shot and killed his former girlfriend and two co-workers at the office's Christmas party.

February 1993, Tampa, Fl.
Paul Calden, an insurance manager fired after a stormy two-year period with Fireman's Fund Insurance Co., walked into a cafeteria where five company executives were lunching. He pulled a handgun from under his coat, and, saying, "This is what you get for firing me," shot all five, killing three and wounding two.

February 1993, Houston, Texas
Upon being fired for theft and harassment, Fernando Ruiz, an employee of Dahn's Fresh Herbs, went to his car and found his semi-automatic pistol. He returned to his boss's office and shot him several times in the upper body, and then turned and shot a co-worker, critically wounding her.

February 1993, Santa Fe Springs, Calif.
Wanda Rodgers, fired from her job as a social worker with the LA County Department of Children's Services, disguised herself with a wig and walked into her former boss's office. She shot her boss in the face and walked out. Her boss was taken to the hospital and stabilized.

February 1993, El Dorado, Ark.
37-year-old Michael Burns opened fire at his place of employment, the Prescolite Lighting plant, apparently because he was upset at being harassed by co-workers. He was stopped only after he was hit on the head with a pipe by another employee. One man was killed in the shooting spree.

April 1993, Dallas, Texas
A former Avis Rent-a-Car employee, fired after an altercation with a co-worker who also had been his girlfriend, returned to the agency and shot her and two others with a .38 caliber semi-automatic handgun.

April 1993, Burlington, N.C.
A disgruntled employee opened fire at the local Winn-Dixie supermarket, killing a co-worker who

allegedly refused to go out with him, and wounding two others.

And everyone knows what happened this past May at two post offices in Michigan and California. Two people died and six were wounded in these May shootings. All told, since 1981 the Post Office has suffered 11 shooting sprees in which 36 people have died.

Chafee puts workplace homicide into terrible and frightening perspective:

> It is a horrifying, and sickening, fact that today, homicide is the number one cause of fatal on-the-job injury for women, and the number three cause for men (behind vehicle accidents and machinery accidents). Think about that: it is murder—not accidents with heavy machinery, falls, poisonings, or motor vehicle accidents—that is the number one cause of death for women on the job! And murder is a major cause of death for men on the job. In fact in 1992 alone, a total of 1,400 men and women were murdered on the job.
>
> What does the National Rifle Association say about this slaughter? After the San Francisco shooting, an NRA spokesman said that calls for gun control were a "sideshow" and that the debate should focus on criminal justice reform to keep violent people in prison.
>
> Well, let me point something out to the NRA. Not only did that gunman in San Francisco buy his three semi-automatic handguns in Nevada—legally—but the FBI says he has no criminal record. And his acquaintances and colleagues, and even his ex-wife, recall him as a "genial" person who "hated

violence." There was no outward indication of his violent intentions, no criminal past; who would have guessed that he was one of what the NRA calls "violent people"?

In virtually every case of "disgruntled employee" shootings, the gun used was a handgun. It's no coincidence and no wonder: there are more than 70 million handguns in the United States, and that number is increasing by 2 million each year. Anyone can get their hands on a handgun. And that includes people with no criminal record, who may be under strain, disgruntled, angry, or drugged, and who with access to these lethal weapons can cause untold human suffering and injury.

Chafee closed with: "I urge my colleagues to join in support of my Public Health and Safety Act."

Waiting periods may well help and I support them, but I do believe that Senator Chafee's approach will lead to a better America.

In the preamble to his legislation he points out that:

- The number of privately held handguns has more than doubled—from 33,000,000 in 1973 to more than 70,000,000 today—in the past two decades alone, and the number of handguns in circulation continues to increase by 2,000,000 handguns each year;
- Handguns play a major role, disproportionate to their number in comparison with rifles and shotguns, in violent crime, intentional and accidental death, and intentional and accidental injury;
- While the number of homicides committed with long guns has remained relatively stable, the number of handgun homicides has set new records every year since 1987,

matching pace with the skyrocketing national homicide rate;

- The number of handgun-related incidents in elementary school and secondary schools has increased sharply, with significant numbers of school children in rural and urban areas reporting easy access to and frequently carrying to school of handguns; and the presence of handguns in school not only provokes worry among parents and children but also causes much-needed school funds to be diverted for purchase of security equipment;
- Handgun violence places considerable strain on the national health care system and is a major contributor to its escalating costs, with at least $4,000,000 being spent annually on emergency care, hospitalization, follow-up care, rehabilitation, and medication;
- Handguns left in the home are of less value than is commonly thought in defending against intruders, and they are far more likely to increase significantly the danger of a handgun fatality or injury to the inhabitants (including children) than to enhance their personal safety;
- Violent crime and injury committed with handguns constitute a burden upon and interference with interstate and foreign commerce, and threaten the domestic tranquility of the nation;

and

- Current Federal firearms policy is wholly inadequate to counteract the social, economic, and financial costs exacted by handguns in our society.

Now, I don't believe that women have a "peaceful" gene that is missing in men, but I think it's realistic to say that women nurture life and perhaps as a result may lead this country to less violent times. I hope that is true. We should start by working for common-sense gun control and making it national policy.

With such a strong lobby in opposition, this will be very difficult to achieve—so we must start now. If you agree, you must lobby your Congressional representatives and join organizations such as The Center to Prevent Handgun Violence. This group is chaired by Sara Brady, whose husband, Jim Brady, was shot along with President Reagan in 1981. The Center works for gun control laws, has a legal fund to counter the lavishly funded gun lobby, provides education for our children so they don't play with or carry guns, and has mobilized to work with the entertainment industry to cut down on violence in entertainment. Also, a new foundation has been set up in the name of John Scully of San Francisco, which will work with other national organizations. For the addresses and phone numbers of these organizations please see the *Appendix* at the back of the book.

The Domestic Agenda will be the focus of the women in the Senate. As women, we want to take care of the world, but to do that we must first take care of our own.

Chapter Nine

The Substance and Politics of Choice

During my campaign for Supervisor in 1971, just before the Supreme Court's 1972 *Roe v. Wade* decision which made a woman's right to choose a federally recognized right in the early stages of her pregnancy, crudely produced leaflets attacking my pro-choice views were handed out against me at Catholic churches. Although the subject of abortion was never brought up in any of the campaign's debates or by any newspaper reporter, each candidate's views were asked in a questionnaire, the results of which were circulated to those religious organizations that were already galvanized on the subject.

I remember being shocked when I saw the written attacks. The choice of whether or not to continue a pregnancy seemed like such a personal issue to me—and a discussion of it so out of place in a County Supervisors race. Supervisors, after all, had nothing to do with making abortion law; that was the province of the state legislature. And the California State Legislature had determined that abortions could be performed only if a doctor filed a report showing that the procedure was necessary for the life or health of the mother of the fetus, should the pregnancy be brought to term.

But whatever the realities of who could make law, the issue was hot. In a close race like mine, in a 40,000-person district, the abortion issue could well have made a difference in the vote, but I ignored it, choosing to focus on the issues that clearly were within the purview of the County Supervisor. That was probably a mistake.

Little did I realize then that being unequivocally pro-choice would spell defeat for me for local office in 1972, but would propel me into the United States Senate 20 years later.

The Issue of Choice in 1992

Pollsters and analysts never identified choice as a deciding factor in my Senate race in 1992, but I think that it was. The pundits underestimated how much the choice issue motivated my supporters. Like no other, my stand on choice led to one of the most effective direct mail campaigns in the country, as well as one of the most dynamic grassroots operations. Pro-choice citizens sent campaign funds, organized, and ultimately, got out the vote on my behalf.

I was very open about my pro-choice views and spoke about choice in almost every speech, even to audiences that didn't expect it. That is because I view reproductive choice as a *freedom* issue, in addition to being a woman's issue. When I speak to groups of men, I frequently challenge them to get involved in the choice battle, saying, "If government can mess with a woman's freedom, government can mess with yours, too!" And besides, I tell them, "You have wives, daughters, and nieces and friends who are counting on you to keep government out of their private lives."

Perhaps as a result, more and more men in California began to see the choice issue in broader terms. Without the support of these men I would not be a United States Senator today. Men who support women candidates deserve a lot of credit, and I thank them every chance that I get.

But in the 1992 campaign, the issue wasn't only my strong history of support for choice; it was also that my opponent was fiercely anti-choice.

Reproductive choice was one of the most sharply defined issues between us, although there were others regarding health care, the environment, and education. While my opponent called *Roe v. Wade* "the craziest decision the Court ever wrote," I called for making it the law of the land. This difference in philosophy was obvious, and every time the Supreme Court narrowed the right to abortion and diminished *Roe*, the issue, for me, took on more of a sense of urgency. My opponent applauded the courts' calling for the outlaw of *Roe*, and I promised to vote to confirm only those Supreme Court nominees who supported the fundamental right of privacy, upon which the right to choose relies.

Pollsters predicted that the *Casey vs. Pennsylvania* decision (June 29, 1992), which set up the test of "undue burden," would be the grand compromise and would knock abortion out as a factor in the race. I never saw it that way, since I viewed *Casey* as a further attack on choice because it affirmed the standing of states to narrow the right to choose. It appears that I was right, because choice remains an issue in elections across America.

So, having served on the Board of Directors of Marin County Planned Parenthood in 1973, and having worked for choice throughout my political career, I had a clear pro-choice history in 1992, and I had an opponent with a history that was just as clearly anti-choice. There was another factor: I was a woman. And because of her gender, a pro-choice woman candidate for the United States Senate becomes a symbol of choice—a constant reminder that the issue of the right to choose has a very human face.

When you look at the campaigns of the women who won the U.S. Senate seats for the first time in 1992, you will see the powerful combination of a strongly pro-choice female versus an anti-choice male that described three of the races. The fourth was a case of a strongly pro-choice woman versus a a man with a weak, waffly record on choice.

Pro-choice Patty Murray, self-described as a "mom in tennis shoes," beat sleek, well-heeled, well-financed, and "mixed-choice" Republican Rod Chandler in Washington State. Pro-choice Democrat Carol Mosely-Braun beat anti-choice Republican Richard Williamson. Pro-choice Dianne Feinstein of California made mincemeat of a weak, allegedly "pro-choice" Republican incumbent, John Seymour, dubbing him "multiple choice" because of his flip-flops on the issue. And I beat Bruce Herschenson, who had rallied the fundamentalist right and who called me "immoral" for my pro-choice views.

I also contend that had Senator Arlen Specter been anti-choice in his views, Democrat Lynn Yeakel would have won her incredible race for the Senate in Pennsylvania, despite Specter's huge spending advantage. I believe that he was able to surmount the effects of his brutal treatment of Anita Hill during the Judiciary Committee hearings on Clarence Thomas only because his support for the right to choose had been clear and consistent.

I believe there is a common thread of indignation that unites a huge number of people against any candidate who treads on an individual's most private decision. America is the land of the free, after all. And I believe that in a nation that has been built on respect for individual rights, such indignation carries across party lines, age differences, gender, income and race differences.

If government is to be truly of, by, and for the people, it must never turn on its people. In this country, religious freedom is cherished, but religion is separate from the government; in fact, our Constitution guarantees the separation of church and state. Any politician who wants government in the middle of this issue is looking for trouble.

Why Choice Matters: The Story I Carry With Me

For many voters, the issue of choice has touched a profoundly personal dimension. They have found that dealing with such a tough decision can be wrenching, even without a government bureaucrat in the middle of it.

In 1963, a decade before *Roe v. Wade* made the news, I was working on Wall Street while putting my husband through law school. I became friendly with a woman colleague, who told me that she was very much in love with her beau. Their relationship was a difficult one, however, and became more difficult when she became pregnant. She very much wanted to have the child with her "boyfriend," but he threw $300 at her and told her to "take care of it."

It was only when she returned to work after being out for about two weeks that she shared her story with me. She described the "dirty back alley" abortion she had had, the fever and bleeding that developed, the fear that she would never again be able to bear a child, the terror of her family finding out, and the ice-cold reaction of the child's "father," who had sent her off by herself, never to talk to her again.

I was stunned. At 21 I was a pretty sheltered person, but I tried hard to lend her courage and strength and shore up her self-esteem. I have never forgotten her story.

An amazing thing happened in 1992. My one-time colleague showed up at my Senate victory party in Washington, D.C. I hadn't seen her since the early '60s, but I had never forgotten her and the hell she went through because abortion was illegal. I don't remember too many acquaintances from those days, but I could never forget her. When we saw each other after all those years, we looked into each other's eyes but did not speak of the secret we shared. Remembering her fears, I was relieved to hear that she was a proud parent, and I know her support for me runs deep.

We cannot go back to the days of darkness again—no matter what obstacles we face and no matter how much energy it takes.

The Ongoing Struggle

I learn every day, and one of the most profound things I have learned is that we cannot believe that a fight has been won forever because it has been won once. We have an obligation to ensure that generations to come understand the kinds of fights for freedom that have been waged.

And you can't leave it to others to do. You have to teach those around you in a personal way, whether the issue is civil rights, the fight for women's equality, the fight to save the environment or the fight to keep politics out of the AIDS crisis. The hardest-won victories can slip away as new demagogues come on the scene, testing for complacency and laxness.

The Freedom of Choice Act

Because the struggle in the courts has been and will continue to be protracted, I believe we must face the issue legislatively. The Freedom of Choice Act is our responsibility and the women of the Senate will lead in that issue. The act must be passed to ensure that a woman can make her choice without government interference either way; whether a woman bears or does not bear a child should not be a decision the government makes. And a woman who is raped must not be forced to bear the rapist's child and must not be denied funding if she is not able to pay for the abortion.

In my view, access to funding for abortion must not be denied to poor women; to do so is to treat them in an unequal and cruel fashion.

I never understood the Supreme Court's reasoning in deciding that the state and federal governments could deny such funding; giving a woman the "right to choose" surely is not a true right if there is no way for her to pay for an abortion. How can this be an equal system of justice? This is why we need the Freedom of Choice Act. And a health care system that includes *all* pregnancy-related procedures, including abortion, in its basic benefits package.

Equal Protection for All

One would have thought that President George Bush would have signed my rape and incest funding amendment which arrived on his desk in 1989. The amendment was known as the Boxer Amendment, authored by Congressman Les AuCoin of Oregon.

Our reasoning was thus: George Bush had been pro-choice in the early years of his political career. Furthermore, he surely wouldn't expect his own child to bear a rapist's child. And since that was the case, we were certain that he would sign this very narrow amendment, which said that if you are poor and raped, you can count on Medicaid funding to pay for an abortion if you choose it. I thought the most compelling argument was made by Congressman Steny Hoyer of Maryland, who reasoned that since candidate George Bush had brought us the rapist Willie Horton in one of the most negative, fear-mongering political ads in history, President George Bush could not expect a woman to bear Willie Horton's child.

But, fearful that he would upset the far right constituency that he always courted, President George Bush vetoed the first pro-choice amendment to pass the House in a decade. Years later, I am still struck by the outrageousness of this—and by George Bush's lack of political courage.

Shackled by Bush's cowardice, we couldn't even protect the neediest and most victimized women in our society— those who had been brutally raped by strangers or by family, and who were too poor to pay for an abortion, a legally sanctioned medical procedure open to women of economic means.

Why We Can't Delay in Passing the Freedom of Choice Act

I fervently disagree with those who say that the need to codify *Roe* in the Freedom of Choice Act is less important these days due to the Court's *Casey* decision.

It is true that the Court, dominated by conservative appointees, didn't outlaw abortion, but its decision in *Casey* has set up an open invitation to the states to place impediments in the way of a woman seeking an abortion, as long as, in the Court's opinion, an "undue burden" is not placed upon her. "Undue burden" is not defined, although the Court found that a 24-hour waiting period, for example, does not constitute an "undue burden." Maybe it doesn't for the Court, but for a woman it certainly can be.

A woman in this predicament thinks about getting an abortion versus bearing the child for days and weeks— non-stop. Subjecting her to a 24-hour waiting period assumes that she is callous and uncaring and unthinking. In my view, government is not only adding a burden; it's insulting her intelligence and conscience.

I agree with Supreme Court Chief Justice Rehnquist when he wrote after *Casey* that *Roe* is just "a shell—like a stage prop without anything behind it." Given the controversy and rancor surrounding this issue, I think that *Casey* sets up a patronizing system that practically invites legislatures to pass laws that attempt to make abortion difficult and nearly impossible. And legislation enacted by these mostly male state legislatures will be reviewed by mostly male judges to see if women are "unduly burdened" by these differing state laws. I trust and hope and believe that we will be strengthened in our right to choose by the addition of Ruth Bader Ginsburg to the Supreme Court.

There is another aspect to *Casey* as well. Why should a woman in Louisiana or Guam be treated differently than a woman from California or New York? The right to choose should be fundamental and guaranteed by federal law. As Senator Barbara Mikulski has said very effectively, "Lincoln didn't free the slaves one plantation at a time; he did it by signing the Emancipation Proclamation." Her point is that this is one nation, and individual rights should be the same state by state, guaranteed at the federal level.

As things stand at present, some states will attempt to place some of the most burdensome obstacles before a woman, and these cases will be litigated, setting up a very confusing array of laws. In many cases, women will be left totally confused about their rights.

On this issue, we need a federal law that will not allow states to treat women so cruelly—the Freedom of Choice Act.

Then we can turn our attention to prevention, so children can stop having children. I believe if we can turn the statistics around here, we will do a tremendous amount to boost our nation's health and economic prosperity. Women in the Senate will focus on this issue and team up with like-minded men to help break the tragic cycle. Surgeon General Jocelyn Elders will be a leader here.

We also need better methods of contraception. Women in the Senate will focus on this issue, as well as on legalization of the use of the drug RU 486, which is not only an alternative to surgical abortion but also a very promising drug for the treatment of breast cancer and Cushing's disease.

Enforcing the Law—Safeguarding Rights

Abortion is legal. Even under this conservative Court, it is still legal; women have the right to a safe and legal abortion—without interference.

In my view, anyone guilty of harassing a doctor who assists a woman in exercising her legal right to an abortion should be found in violation of federal law. Similarly, anyone preventing a woman from entering a family planning clinic where abortion is performed should be found in violation of federal law. In my view, anyone situated on federal property and anyone who uses the phones or the mail to stalk either a woman seeking an abortion or a doctor or health care professional who is involved in abortion should be found in violation of federal law.

It certainly is obvious to many people that the use of the term "pro-life" to describe those who would commit such harassment and violence against people is the cruelest irony; and the use of the term "pro-life" to describe a position which would lead to dangerous illegal abortions and thus to needless death is another irony.

What about the doctors and their children and their families? They also deserve to have their lives protected.

In the years since *Roe*, we have seen the burning of clinics, acids thrown into clinics, harassment of health professionals and women seeking legal health care. Then with the killing of Dr. David Gunn in Pensicola, Florida in March of 1993, the abortion debate took an even uglier and more brutal turn.

Each and every citizen on either side of the choice issue must now speak out.

Those who belong to the anti-abortion movement can help by resigning from organizations that do not speak out clearly against violence. Saying that "killing is wrong" but is justified because "these doctors kill life" is not speaking out against violence. The message must be clear.

Those who belong to the pro-choice movement must let physicians and health care providers know that they are respected for their courage and that those physicians who go into family planning practice should be applauded for doing so.

The Real World

The challenge is to stop abortions by stopping unwanted pregnancies. But until the perfect contraception is found, there will be unwanted pregnancies. We must approach life as it *is*, not as we wish it were.

We must work to make things better, not to punish our people if they err. To err is human; to punish for unwanted pregnancy is inhumane.

We must understand that Americans have different views on the subject of abortion and that those views should be respected.

Demagogues must not push people toward violence. When anti-abortion groups paint doctors as "the butchers of mankind," they must also take responsibility for the violence they sow.

The man arrested for the murder of Dr. David Gunn in Pensicola had a history of violence and had viewed several graphic anti-abortion movies before he shot the doctor three times in the chest.

The man who showed the graphic anti-abortion films to Dr. Gunn's killer compared himself to a "general" who "can't control it if one [of the troops] goes bad." In an interview with the *New York Times* he said, "I can't be responsible."

I believe that we need more responsibility in this society. I believe that if you incite someone to violence you must assume responsibility for his acts.

As the violence escalates, health care officials will be dissuaded from providing legal abortions. And as fewer and fewer doctors perform abortions, it may not matter if *Roe v. Wade* becomes codified into law; there won't be anyone left who is willing to step forward and perform the abortions. This may well be the goal of the anti-abortion movement—but it must not be tolerated.

It is time for America to turn against people who incite violence. It is time for America to turn against those who would put the faces of doctors who perform legal abortions on "most wanted" posters. America must turn away from domestic terrorism.

As columnist Ellen Goodman argued in a *Washington Post* article on March 13, 1993, "Michael Griffin [Dr. Gunn's killer] cannot just become the next logical step in the escalator of violence. He must be the last step."

Women in the Senate will work to see that this escalation of violence around the choice issue ends by strongly supporting and advocating for Senator Kennedy's Freedom of Access to Clinics bill and anti-stalking legislation.

We understand that the real targets of these fanatical groups are the women who seek abortions. If a doctor is called a "baby killer" ("Praise God," a "pro-life" protester said about the Gunn slaying, "one of the killers is dead"), then don't you think that these people believe that women are partners in that killing? In the past, such fanatics called for imprisoning the women seeking abortion; when the public expressed its outrage at this, they shifted their attack to doctors. But once the doctors have been scared off, they will return to the women, leaving them in a dangerous situation, without access to safe abortions.

The drug RU 486, providing a non-surgical alternative to abortion, may well be the only way to keep abortion private—and thus not subject to outside interference. That is why the anti-abortion groups are so committed to keeping the drug out of the country after its successful testing in France and England. Pro-choice Americans must rally to the defense of the drug companies that seek to begin distributing it in our country, fighting the boycotts and demonstrations that pro-life forces are sure to organize.

A Clear Choice

Let us be very clear about the issue of choice. It isn't about being pro-abortion. The perfect method of contraception does not yet exist. And so, we must make sure that the right to choose remains an individual woman's choice, rather than that of the government, the judiciary, the religious right—or the members of a violent mob outside a clinic.

Chapter Ten

Save the Children

"If our American way of life fails the child, it fails us all."
—Pearl S. Buck, The Child Who Never Grew

Women in the Senate will be a voice for those who cannot fly to the Capitol to lobby, or hire high-priced lobbyists to plead their case. Women in the Senate will be a voice for the most vulnerable of all our citizens—our children.

I don't believe that women Senators will be children's advocates simply because it is the right thing to do—although it is; not just because it is the moral thing to do—although it is; nor because many of us are moms—although many of us are. It's more than that. Women will be advocates for children because it makes common sense. In plain English: the economic and social future of our nation depends on how well our children are doing today.

How anyone in public life can't see this is beyond me. It shouldn't take a Ph.D. in anything to "get it."

Our children are in trouble and the warning signs cannot be ignored.

The state of many of our children today reminds me of the little canaries the coal miners used to take down to the mines. They watched these canaries to make sure that the air was healthful for them to breathe. When the canaries started to struggle and finally succumbed, it meant that everyone should clear out of the mine.

Real Economics

Well, children are struggling today—too many of them—and that is a preview of what is ahead, a sign of a troubled society. That's the bad news. The good news is that we can turn it around without bankrupting our country. As a matter of fact we can't afford *not* to turn it around.

I believe the most cost-effective thing we can do to put a stop to the problems in our society is to save the children.

If we save the children—invest relatively modest amounts of our country's treasure in our children—then we will save countless dollars. And unlike the miners who had to evacuate, we will be able to enjoy our country whether we happen to be in the cities or the suburbs or out in the country.

The facts are so obvious. Physically healthy people don't need costly crisis intervention in hospital emergency rooms, and mentally healthy people, people who believe in themselves and in the American dream, will not turn to gangs and drugs and crime.

We all know it costs more to send a teenager to jail for a year than it does to send him or her to Harvard. That doesn't mean that we will send every child to Harvard or even that every child has to go on to college. It illustrates very clearly, though, that the price of neglect is enormous . . . we pay dearly later for the problems of neglect.

Here's a stark figure. Every crop of high school dropouts costs America over 100 billion dollars over their lifetimes . . . every crop . . . every year. Talk about balancing the budget! In ten years that's almost one trillion dollars—almost the size of the federal budget.

There is no doubt in my mind that the one thing we can do to make our society better, more peaceful, more competitive, is to *save the children*. If there is one thing we can and should do to cut down on the outrageous costs of burglary, homicide, prisons, drug treatment, AIDS babies, crack babies, premature babies, broken families, abusive families . . . it's *save the children*.

A Portrait of Our Children

Let's take a look at our children. Their status has been studied and described by many organizations.

In their booklet, "The State of America's Children: 1992," the Children's Defense Fund asks this question: "Is this the best America can do?" They then answer with the following facts:

- Every 12 seconds of the school day, an American child drops out (380,000 a year).
- Every 13 seconds, an American child is reported abused or neglected (2.7 million a year).
- Every 26 seconds, an American child runs away from home (1.2 million a year).
- About every minute, an American teenager has a baby.
- Every nine minutes, an American child is arrested for a drug offense.
- Every 40 minutes, an American child is arrested for drunk driving.
- Every 53 minutes in our rich land, an American child dies from poverty.
- Every three hours, a child is murdered.

The United States has:

- An infant mortality rate higher than 19 other countries.
- A higher infant mortality rate for black infants than the overall rates of 31 other nations, including Cuba, Bulgaria and Kuwait.
- A death rate among pre school children worse than 19 other nations.
- A worse low birth-weight rate than 30 other nations.
- A low birth-weight rate among blacks worse than the overall rates of 73 other countries, including many third World and former Communist Eastern Bloc countries.
- A smaller portion of babies immunized against polio than 16 other nations. (On June 6, 1993 the United Nations Children's Fund, UNICEF, said that the U.S. trails many developing African and Latin American countries in vaccination rates for children under the age of two.)
- A smaller proportion of non-white babies immunized against polio than the overall rate of 69 other nations.
- A ranking of 12 out of 14 among industrialized nations in science achievement among 13-year-olds.
- A ranking of 13 out of 14 among industrialized nations in mathematics among 13-year-olds.
- A higher child poverty rate than seven other industrialized western countries. One in five U.S. children—14.3 million—are poor, making them the poorest group of Americans.

Our nation has:

- An estimated 2.4 million children involved in juvenile prostitution every year.
- The highest rate of working children among affluent countries, according to the National Consumers League.

- The highest rate of teen drug use of any nation in the industrialized world, according to the U.S. Department of Heath and Human Services.

And the U.S. is on record as being one of seven countries carrying out the capital punishment of juvenile offenders within the past decade. At least 145 nations ban such executions; we have executed more juvenile offenders than any nation except for Iran and Iraq.

The Children's Defense Fund profiles poor children in America. Out of 100 poor children in America:

- Forty are white non-Latino.
- Thirty-four are African-American.
- Twenty-two are Latino.
- Five are Asian, Pacific Islander, Native American or Alaskan Native.
- Thirty-seven live in families headed by married couples.
- Fifty-nine live in female-headed households.
- Four live in male-headed households.
- Sixty-two live in families with at least one worker.
- Seventeen live in families with two or more workers.
- Twenty-two live with families with at least one full-time, year-round worker.
- Forty-five live in central cities.
- Thirty-two live in the suburbs.
- Twenty-four live in rural areas.
- Forty-four live with families with incomes of less than half the poverty level—about $7,000 for a family of four.
- Forty are younger than six.
- Eleven live in families headed by persons under 25 years old.

Cost-Effective Measures

If we made a determination to ensure that our children are healthy regardless of the circumstances into which they are born, our society would make a major step forward—and it makes economic sense. President Clinton wants to expand free vaccinations to all children whose families can't afford them and he wants to make certain that every American, regardless of age, has health insurance. I know that Democratic women in the Senate will help him attain his goal.

We know that every dollar we spend on childhood immunization saves $10 in medical costs later. That fact was brought home to me in the late '80s, when I held hearings in San Diego, Calif. as the Chair of the Budget Committee's Task Force on Health. The director of the San Diego Children's Hospital told me about a case where the county medical department wound up spending $800,000 to save a child's life who came down with the measles, because the child never got his measles shots. At the time the shot would have cost $14. The sad fact is that the child died.

Medically and economically, we know that prevention works. For example: one dollar spent on comprehensive maternity care for pregnant women saves $3.38 in later costs in health care problems avoided for mother and child. Another $3.13 is saved for each dollar invested in the special supplemental food program for Women, Infants and Children (WIC). This program of nutrition and food counseling for pregnant women and provision of decent food for infants and children cuts the incidence of low birth-weight babies and the incredibly costly care they require. These are all proven programs, and yet, it is a never-ending fight to obtain full funding.

Immunizations, pre-natal care and the WIC program will get children off to a healthy start *and* will save dollars in the long run. When Congressman George Miller was chairman of the Select Committee on Children, Youth and Families he brought these statistics out over and over again to the Reagan and Bush Administrations, but they didn't seem to care. At last we have President Bill Clinton—who understands this.

And he's backed by more than child advocacy groups. The Government Accounting Office (GAO), which is the investigative arm of the Congress, confirmed recently that the WIC program saves three dollars for every dollar spent. "WIC cost $296 million in 1990 and it saved state and local government and health care providers $853 million in the babies first year and more than $1 billion over 18 years," reports the GAO. "Women and children who take advantage of WIC show improved health and nutrition, thus eliminating the need for costly health care from problems associated with poor nutrition and inadequate health counseling, during pregnancy and early childhood."

WIC: The Prototype for Success

In their report entitled "WIC: A Success Story," the Food and Research Action Center, funded by the Ford and the Prudential Foundations, found that the WIC program leads to ten benefits. These are:

- WIC reduces deaths and infant mortality.
- WIC reduces low birth-weight rates and increases the duration of pregnancy.
- WIC improves the growth of at-risk infants and children.
- WIC decreases the incidence of iron deficiency anemia in children.

- WIC improves the dietary intake of pregnant and post-partum women and improves weight gain in pregnant women.
- Pregnant women participating in WIC receive pre-natal care earlier.
- Children enrolled in WIC are more likely to have a regular source of medical care and are better immunized.
- Children who receive WIC benefits demonstrate superior cognitive development.
- WIC significantly improves children's diets.
- WIC is cost-effective.

The idea for the WIC program was sparked in 1968, when it became clear that women who had inadequate diets during pregnancy had a higher risk of miscarriages and other health problems. Without adequate nutrition during the mother's pregnancy, infants were found to have lower birth-weights, smaller head sizes, and stunted growth. So the government provided free commodities to at-risk pregnant women as well as to new mothers and children under the age of six.

The program was a success, so in 1972 Congress authorized WIC for three years. More success followed and the program has continued year after year, although not at full funding.

For the cost of approximately $30, a monthly package of food containing protein, iron, calcium and vitamins A and C is provided. The foods include cereal, formula, milk, eggs, cheese, orange juice, dried beans, and peanut butter. Nutrition education is also given—which is a very important part of the program, not only because of what participants learn about nutrition, but because of other information they glean about parenting.

Now here's the crazy part: only half of those eligible participate in WIC. 4.5 million women, infants and children participate—but millions more need nutritional assistance.

We know that a child's nutritional health begins with pregnancy and early infancy. If this nutrition is missing, the loss is reflected in less successful school performance, lower intelligence, and physical and developmental handicaps.

Democratic women in the Senate support full funding— and will be of great help to the men in the Senate, such as Ted Kennedy and Pat Leahy, who have been fighting for full funding for WIC for years.

Cutting Down on Premature Births

During my campaign for U.S. Senate, I often visited hospitals to learn about health care issues. I was always drawn to the premature infant wards. My staff learned that I could not stay away and I told them why: both my children had been born prematurely. In those days—the '60s—prematurity was clearly a life-threatening situation, because much of the technology present in "preemie" wards today did not exist then. I remember being told that my son had a 50/50 chance of making it because his lungs were immature. I also remember praying while looking at him from afar. In those days you couldn't touch a preemie unless you were the nurse or doctor. So for one month I couldn't hold Doug. In those days it was up to the baby to make it—and it was up to God. Today more of those tiny babies make it because of great advances in technology.

The preemie wards in hospitals across the country are places of miracles. I've held some of those miracles—two pound babies, drug-addicted babies—and I've choked up and vowed over and over to do what I could do to help.

Unlike my babies, whose prematurity was the result of my body's inability to hold the pregnancies much beyond seven months, these babies are born suffering because of a lack of pre-natal care—a lack of clear-cut education on the dangers of drug and alcohol and tobacco use during pregnancy, and a lack of clear-cut education on the importance of family planning and contraception.

Teenagers having babies are really children having children—a situation we must remedy if we are to save the next generation.

Slightly more than one million teenagers—about the equivalent of the entire population of San Antonio, Texas—got pregnant in 1989.

After declining from the early '70s, the teen birth rate started to increase in 1987. In 1989 there were 58.1 births per 1,000 women ages 15 to 19. About one in every 17 women in that age group gave birth in 1989—the highest rate since 1973. Almost two-thirds of all births to teens are to unmarried girls, compared with less than one-third in 1970.

Violence and Victimization

But teenage pregnancy is not the only problem. Another is violence.

In 1989, 6,185 young people between the ages of 15 and 24 were homicide victims—that's 17 per day! They represent 16 times more casualties from violence here at home than were total casualties from Desert Shield and Desert Storm in 1990 and 1991.

Since 1988 American teenage boys generally have been more likely to die from gunshot wounds than from all natural causes combined, according to the National Center for Health Statistics. Almost 1.9 million teenagers were the victims of violent crimes in 1990.

Substance Abuse

In 1990 almost one-quarter of surveyed 12- to 17-year-olds and more than half of 18- to 25-year-olds reported having used illicit drugs (drugs other than alcohol and tobacco) at some time in their lives. These figures do not include information from runaway, incarcerated, or homeless youths, who are at greatest risk of drug abuse.

Sixty to seventy percent of all teenagers try alcohol by age 15, and more than 30 percent of high school seniors say they have engaged in binge drinking within the previous two weeks—that is, they had five or more drinks in a row. The costs of such abuse—in dollars and in heartache—are enormous. Now we hear about a new startling development—youngsters "sniffing" ordinary household items to get high.

Education

In 1990 more than 14 percent of 18 and 19-year-olds had not graduated from high school and were not in school, a percentage that has remained roughly stable for the last decade, despite an increasing demand for better-educated employees in the work force.

More than 62 percent of 1990-1991 high school graduates were enrolled in college in October 1991—the highest ratio ever. But the figures suggest that only a small portion will receive bachelor's degrees within six years. Among 1980 high school graduates, 27 percent of Asians, 20 percent of whites, ten percent of blacks, and seven percent of Latinos had completed a bachelor's degree by 1986. Clearly, we have to make a better case for higher education—and make higher education more accessible to all our young people.

Employment And Income

In 1991 nearly one in five teenagers (18.6 percent) active-ly looking for work could not find a job.

The average annual earnings of 20- to 24-year-old men in 1990 totaled only $10,241, which is just below the pover-ty level for a family of three. For women in the same age group, average annual earnings were much lower—a mere $7,242.

These figures do not present a pretty picture—and when these teens have babies, as one million of them do each year, the situation worsens markedly. It is absolutely necessary to break this cycle of poverty, low self-esteem and school drop-out rates in order to brake all the other problems that follow.

The place to start is with each child in the pre-natal stage.

Voices of Commitment

I am not suggesting that we forget about those who have fallen through the cracks in the last 12 years. We should back Congresswoman Maxine Waters' idea of stipend programs for 17- through 30-year-olds who have lost their way.

Maxine Waters of Los Angeles is a real champion of the young people who are the products of the last decade of neglect. After the Rodney King trial, and the riots that followed, she really put her heart and soul into reaching out to those that too many have given up on.

Before the federal trial, which was the second trial of the police officers that had beaten King, Maxine went out into the community where most feared to tread. Everyone was afraid of another uprising if the second verdict matched the first acquittal verdict, but Maxine refused to give up on these young people. While others spent their time making sure the police were battle-ready, Maxine Waters made sure that these young people heard from her that they were important and that their lives were meaningful.

She wrote a heart-felt letter that was hand delivered to more than 200,000 people in her inner-city Los Angeles Congressional district. It read in part:

> This Rodney King thing is a mother! It has gotten to all of us. The beating was savage! The cops were dead wrong but the Reginald Denny beating was wrong too! Now we have the trials of Rodney King and the L.A. Four.
>
> The killing and the violence must stop! Too many have died already. You have got to live—not die! Life is too precious.
>
> The news media wants to whip us into a frenzy. Did you see the picture that *USA Today* had on its front page? Brothers with guns in their hands with the caption, "L.A. Uneasy." It was a bogus, set-up photograph. The brothers thought they were turning in their guns for jobs and thought the photo would help them. *USA Today* apologized for the photo and disciplined the editor involved.
>
> Everywhere, journalists—from the *L.A. Times,* the *New York Times,* the *Wall Street Journal* and the *Washington Post*—are asking, "Is there going to be another riot?" I think there are those who want to see death and destruction.
>
> TIME OUT! Let us work for justice. Let us keep our voices loud for the selection of representative juries and fair court proceedings.
>
> Let us speak up! Let us get the ministers and politicians to speak up! Let us learn how to rally and protest! Let us read and keep up with the facts!

We must let the world know we are not going anywhere! This is our city and our community. We have got to make it right. We've got to *build*, not burn. We've got to *live*, not die.

To do this work we've *got* to live! We cannot be killed nor can we kill. We cannot risk our lives nor the lives of others.

When the verdicts come down, there will be thousands of police, sheriffs, and national guards on the streets. If you take to the streets with a molotov cocktail in your hand, a gun in your belt or a brick ready to throw, you give the police the legal right to kill you.

Our anger and frustration must not drive us into the streets. We must use our minds and our God-given talents and our legacy of perseverance and struggle. We fight our battles in the courtroom and the halls of power. We must organize and rally and protest. And, through it all, we will celebrate *living*— not *dying!*

I wish we could make life better for everyone, today, now. I wish we all had jobs, and happy, loving experiences each day of our lives. I wish we had peace of mind. And, if I could, I would give it to you.

Each day brings a new opportunity—a new possibility. I love you and I will fight for you. I need you to stand with me to make this a better place. Let us get smart—it's time to chill!

From Me to You With Love,
Maxine Waters

Maxine "gets" it. She will not turn her back on these young people. As a mother and a grandmother, she will not sit back and do nothing. She prods, she pushes, she speaks with clarity and passion, and sometimes with anger. Maxine has no time to waste. She embodies the power of commitment, the power of knowledge, and the power of the streets.

But women have a new way of showing their power. It is shown in direct, sometimes defiant, talk. It was shown when the seven women members of Congress walked over to the Senate, not worrying about the Senate's etiquette. The power of women prods the establishment and ruffles feathers and often doesn't get good press or good editorials. But people know that Maxine Waters—and women like her—will fight for them.

Women in politics are fighters because there's no time to waste. And nowhere in America will people see this fighting spirit more than they will see it on behalf of the children.

Bringing the Children Out of the Shadows

In April of 1993, the *New York Times* ran a series of articles called "Children of the Shadows"—moving portraits of ten young people. The headlines each day gave a clue to their stories. In "First Born, Fast Grown: The Manful Life of Nicholas, 10," reporter Isabel Wilkenson writes of Nicholas: "He is nanny, referee, housekeeper, handyman . . . sometimes up past midnight, mopping floors and washing the children's school clothes in the bathtub. It is a nightly chore: the children have few clothes and wear the same thing every day."

Another story reads, "Fear and Ghosts: The World of Marcus, 19." This is the story of a boy who is one of ten children with an absent father. The profile notes that the mother of a friend of Marcus has offered him sex for five dollars—so she can buy crack. He told reporter Don Terry,

"If you ain't careful, living around here can drive you crazy."

Day after day, story after story can bring a feeling of nearly overwhelming helplessness as one realizes the odds facing these young people. But we can never feel helpless in life. That is not why we are here.

As the *New York Times* editorial stated on April 25, 1993: "These children of the shadows are definitely trying to make it while fighting tremendous odds. . . . Private individuals can do a lot. But rebuilding the safety net of services that was badly neglected over the last decade is a public responsibility, and opportunity. . . . Society has a choice. Keep these children in the shadows or bring them out into the light."

We must bring these children out of the shadows—or at least try. It will not be easy, because they have missed the foundation of love and learning already. But there is no reason we cannot ensure that a child born from this day forward never gets into the shadows in the first place.

We may never have a perfect record, but we must aim for one. In ways large and small, we need to honor each child. Here's my plan:

1. **Teenage pregnancy prevention** through education and counseling beginning in junior high school. Ensure that health-care reform includes health clinics in high schools.
2. **Pre-natal care** for pregnant women through a health-care system that reaches all of our people.
3. **Full funding of WIC programs.**
4. **Immunizations for all our children.** According to James Grant, the head of Unicef: "Calcutta, Lagos (Nigeria) and Mexico City have far higher levels of immunization of children ages one and two than do New York City, Washington D.C., or even the United States as a whole."

5. **"15-month Houses,"** a plan by Senator Bill Bradley of New Jersey to provide very young or low-income mothers with health care, parenting education, substance abuse counseling if needed, and education or vocational training. While providing a safe residential home for mother and child and by providing pediatric care and nutrition and cognitive stimulation (exercises with shapes, sounds and colors) for the child, this plan has been tested successfully in several cities, including La Casita in the South Bronx. The Robert Wood Johnson Foundation has compared children who have received this type of early start with those who did not. They found that children who had this type of start had many fewer behavior and learning problems later in childhood.

6. **Full Funding of Head Start.** A comprehensive preschool program that prepares children to enter school ready to learn, this proven 28-year-old program combines learning with social services and parental involvement so crucial to children of pre-school age. This is another program that saves three dollars for every dollar spent, as children who get that "head start" have a much lower rate of educational failure, teen pregnancy, welfare dependency, and crime. The "Children Now" organization, in its 1993 Federal Legislative Agenda for California's children, points out that only 24 percent of California's eligible children can get into Head Start programs. Nationwide, the participation level is about one-third. Put another way, of the 1.7 million three- and four-year-olds eligible for Head Start in 1991, only 621,000 can presently be accommodated.

The current level of low funding makes no sense, if we are to believe a new long-term study released by the High Scope Educational Research Foundation and reported by the *New York Times* on April 20, 1993. The study showed that children who go through Head Start have better earnings, more stable marriages, and fewer drug problems, among other advantages.

Of course, Head Start is not perfect; advocates are working to improve the program as it expands. Some say the advantages of Head Start fade as children reach ten years of age. But I contend that the fading advantage is not Head Start's fault so much as the fall-off of excellent programs as children get older. Therefore, I also recommend:

7. **Quality child care programs.** With 67% of mothers with children younger than 18 in the civilian labor force, and 53% of women with an infant younger than one in the labor force, there is a great need for adequate child care in addition to Head Start, which is a pre-school program.

On-site child care at or near the job should be encouraged. I have visited many of these facilities and know that they really help workforce morale. The use of schools for after-school programs should be encouraged. (When my children were young several of us founded a program called the Kentfield After-Care Center so that we could cut down on the number of so-called latchkey kids—children who were left alone after school. This program is still operating, administered by a non-profit corporation with fees on a sliding scale. It started about 16 years ago and is extremely successful. A young child left alone after school means television and, maybe, trouble.)

8. **Mentoring programs,** where youths are matched with adults who provide role models for them during the tough, at-risk years, should become the quality bridge between Head Start and high school.

I would like to see funding for mentors who are in junior college, to help them raise the dollars they need to pay rising tuition costs. In this way, they can be rewarded for working with youngsters who will look up to them.

Mentoring is a perfect project for National Youth Service, for sororities and fraternities, for corporations and for senior citizens.

We should mobilize our country. Everyone who cares should give a child a little time, a little caring, and a little tutoring on school subjects and on life.

I also feel that special attention should be given to mentor matches where the adult is a young adult, as in the program discussed in the *Washington Post* on May 9, 1990. "Four times a week Vanessa Cardenas, 15, listens to the heartache and frustration of 11- and 12-year-old Spanish-speaking children, like herself," writes reporter Jane Seaberry. She points out that school mentors are more than tutors, "helping youngsters with personal and non-academic problems and sometimes planning activities outside of school."

Of course, adult mentor programs are less risky—and also very beneficial. A study in public/private mentors in Philadelphia reported in *Education Week* in August of 1992 focused on 26 mentor pairs and found that the "majority of relationships flourished."

I know from personal experience that mentoring is a way to make a difference in a child's life, to reach into the goodness of a child and of yourself at the same time. When I first moved to San Francisco in 1965, and after I had my first child, I volunteered for a program called "The Education Auxiliary." I went into a classroom in a tough neighborhood once a week and worked with a few children who needed extra help. I also took them out of the classroom; I read to them and talked to them and listened to them. It helped the teachers a great deal, it made the children feel special, and I felt very good about it.

9. **School Reform.** I'm not an expert in the ways to teach, although I spend a great deal of time visiting schools and trying to teach. But I know one thing . . . a good teacher is

the key. But even the greatest teacher needs help—like manageable class sizes, decent supplies, and community and parental involvement. And in this age of computers, our children must have access to these incomparable teaching tools.

In the '50s Congress passed the National Defense Education Act. The Russians had just launched Sputnik and we feared that we had fallen behind in science and math. So the federal government developed a targeted math and science program that was locally administered. It went on for a decade, with excellent results.

I think it's time for another such act. I'd like to see us target our new effort at class size, making the physical plant attractive again, and putting computers in the classroom, to name a few ideas. President Clinton and Secretary of Education Richard Riley have a good track record on education reform and I look forward to working with them on this issue.

As a product of public education from kindergarten through college, I believe that a great public school system is the heart of America. It has always been the great equalizer—one way that each of us could get our opportunity to shine. I'm proud of my public education, and I will work toward a time when every American can say the same. I am the first U.S. Senator to graduate from Brooklyn College, but I hope I'm not the last. Brooklyn College gave me an almost free college degree!

And important as academics are, I believe that school reform should also include vocational training. Not every person can or should go on to college. When I was a kid in the '50s, "voc. ed." meant welding and shop and working on cars. Today it should mean that and more, including bio-technology training, chefs' courses, training for travel agents and for computer operators.

President Clinton sees a youth apprenticeship program for the 40 percent of those who don't go on to college. I think it's a wonderful possibility. We have a superb network of community colleges throughout the country that could serve as the high school-to-work transition.

Our trading partners Germany and Japan, who are our biggest competitors, both train their skilled work force. In America, it's a matter of luck if any young students get training. The irony is that vocational education in America began in 1917 in response to advances in German and Japanese productivity and got another boost when America feared the same two countries' boosts in productivity in the '30s. Education experts point out that this is the third time through the cycle in this century.

It seems to me that voc. ed. should no longer be the "ugly duckling" of our school system. We need a skilled workforce in too many areas to ignore voc. ed.'s potential. 10. **National Service**. President Clinton has proposed a fine program to assist our young people with college tuition in exchange for national service. He explained it very clearly at Rutgers University in New Jersey on March 1, 1993:

> National service will be America at its best, building community, offering opportunity, and rewarding responsibility. National service is a challenge for Americans from every background and walk of life. And it values something far more than money. National service is nothing less than the American way to change America. It is rooted in the concept of community, the simple idea that none of us on our own will ever have as much to cherish about our own lives if we are out here all alone as we will if we work together, that somehow society really is an organism in which the whole can be greater than the

sum of its parts. And every one of us, no matter how many privileges with which we are born, can still be enriched by the contributions of the least of us, and that we will never fulfill our individual capacities until, as Americans, we can be what God meant for us to be. If that is so, if that is true, my fellow Americans, and you believe it, it must therefore follow that each of us has an obligation to serve, for it is perfectly clear that all of us cannot be what we ought to be until those of us who can help others—and that is nearly all of us—are doing something to help others live up to their potential. The concept of community and the idea of service are as old as our history.

The National Service plan that I propose will be built on the same principles as the old GI bill. When people give something of invaluable merit to their country, they ought to be rewarded with the opportunity to further their education. National service will challenge people to do the work that should, and indeed must be done, and cannot be done unless the American people voluntarily give themselves up to that work. It will invest in the future of every person who serves.

We'll ask young people all across the country, and some who aren't so young, who want to further their college education, to serve in our schools as teachers or tutors in reading and mathematics. We'll ask you to help our police forces across the nation, training members for a new police corps that will walk beats and work with neighborhoods and build the kind of community ties that will prevent crime from happening in the first place so that our police officers won't have to spend all their time chasing criminals. I'll ask young people to work to help control pollution and recycle wastes, to paint darkened buildings, and clean up neighborhoods—to work with senior citizens and combat homelessness and help children in trouble get out of it and build a better life. And these are just a few of the things that you will be able to do. . . .

National service is a concept that will give meaning to the lives of many young men and women. They will be educated, they will use their education to make our country better, and they will be enriched by the process. I am proud to say that the House and Senate passed the National Service bill and President Clinton signed it into law in September, 1993.

So there it is, from pre-natal care to national service. My contention is that a plan like this for the children will turn our nation around.

A Passion for Children

To answer the legitimate question of how we pay for this type of comprehensive plan: I believe we need to readjust our priorities—from the civilian side of the budget—as well as the military side. But I also would like to point out that should we undertake to reach these priorities in a sound and businesslike fashion, the program will be more than paid for with far lower incidence of childhood disease, with far lower infant mortality rates, with a far lower teenage pregnancy rate, with a far lower alcoholism rate, with a far lower abortion rate, with a far lower divorce rate, with a far lower school drop-out rate, with a far lower welfare rate, with a higher productivity rate, and with far higher revenues into the treasury as more people are working. A far lower deficit will follow. Truly, the major cause of our deficit is unemployment and a draw-down on the social safety net programs that follow. If we can solve the intractable problems of poverty, helplessness, and crime, we will recover from the moral and fiscal deficit. And it all starts with our children.

My special project as a United States Senator is staying in touch with the young people of California. Every time I'm in the state, I do all I can to speak to classes of students. It is clear to me that by the time they are juniors and seniors in high schools the die has been cast for their futures. You can see it on their faces—many of them are so cynical that they believe in absolutely nothing that is meant to give them hope or to help them dream. Their lives have been so bereft of hope and so filled with disappointment that they don't dare let any optimism in.

But every once in a while I reach some of those students. So can you.

If there is anything we must do as women in the Senate, and women in politics, it is to turn around the neglect of our children. Some of the men in politics are already there, like Congressman George Miller, who founded the Select Committee on Children, Youth and Families, and all through the '80s, taught us all about the cost effectiveness of many of the issues I have discussed in this chapter.

But sadly, there are many men who only have passion for B-2 bombers and high-tech military projects. I remember one of my colleagues in the House of Representatives declaring in an emotional voice what a disgrace it was that the women of this nation spent more on panty-hose than the country spent on Star Wars (although we spent more on Star Wars than any other weapons system). I couldn't believe how upset he was. I took to the floor and told him not to worry so much: at more than 3 billion dollars, Star Wars was funded beyond anyone's wildest dreams. (Anyway, I said, there's a reason why the women of America spend so much on panty-hose. Unlike Star Wars, panty-hose are reliable and cost-effective. And most important, panty-hose don't change their mission every day, like Star Wars! I guess I learned from Schroeder that a sense of humor could make a point.) Now, if I could just get this guy as excited about the need to save the children!

As women in politics, we must reach out to our male colleagues to explain in economic terms why the children are so important. And if they've never done it, we should take them to a premature baby ward and have them see for themselves the sheer stupidity of neglect, then take them to a Head Start program to see the utter common-sense of investment.

I know of no politician who has never said, in one way or another, that our future depends on our children. We certainly have plenty of politicians who can't wait to find a microphone in the House and Senate to talk about the importance of saving a fetus. (As Congressman Barney Frank of Massachusetts once told me, "Some of these guys fight like hell for your right to be born, but after that, you're on your own!") It doesn't make much sense.

We are losing our children, and to stand by and let it happen when you are in a position to do something about it is unforgivable . . . whether you're a Democrat or a Republican. The women of the Senate know this, and we will take action.

The women of the Senate have much to do, and saving our children is at the top of the list.

PART IV

MOVING TOWARD
THE FUTURE

Chapter Eleven

Women in the Senate: The 50 Percent Solution

I do not believe in quotas. I do believe that the nation would be better served if there were more women in the Senate. I'll settle for 50 percent.

It's not that I believe that women are better than men, but our perspective is surely different. And if America is to solve the problems facing it, we need *all* perspectives.

The Value of Different Perspectives

In the last 20 years, psychologists have written dozens of books about the different way men and women communicate. I really don't know why we have these differences, but I do know that both approaches are needed in the Senate.

Two issues clearly demonstrate the difference in men's and women's approaches: the passage of anti-stalking legislation and the dilemma of gays in the military.

A shocking number of women in this country—experts put the number at more than 100,000—have been "stalked"—threatened and pursued by an unstable individual—but it took putting women into the Senate to get the problem taken seriously. In 1993, I was able to bring anti-stalking legslation to the "new" Senate Judiciary, which thanks to Senator Joe Biden, now has two women on it. Senators Dianne Feinstein and Carol Moseley-Braun strongly supported the bill because they themselves had been stalked. They brought that perspective to the Senate.

Senator Feinstein related her story to the committee:

> I have been . . . the victim of stalking, and it is an interesting story because it also accompanies mental instability of someone who, while I was mayor, made some threats, believes I killed his mother, had prior weapons charges, went to State prison, had a psychiatric report that he should not be released, was released, had an order not to make any contact with me or my office, did make contact, went back to prison.
>
> They will hold him as long as they can and then he will be released again. Now, this is somebody, unless treatment has really made a difference, who is going to continue on with this same pattern.

Senator Moseley-Braun, too, had been stalked—by an employee whom she had fired.

Too many women are stalked. Too many women are beaten. Too many women are raped. Too many women are harassed. And women in the Senate will make sure these problems receive new and much-needed attention.

The other issue that brought the difference in men's and women's perspectives to the fore was the debate about gays in the military. Now, I'll admit from the start that I feel this should have been a non-issue: gays and lesbians have served in the military for as long as anyone can remember, so why continue the charade, why continue the witch-hunt and the harassment of patriotic Americans doing their job?

A constituent of mine brought the issue home to me. A physician who had served in World War II, he was visiting me in my Capitol Hill office on another issue. I asked him his opinion of the controversy.

"Barbara," he said, "I was on the front lines during World War II. I can tell you unequivocally that there were gays in my unit. And I can say with the utmost honesty that I didn't care if the person next to me was gay or straight as long as he could shoot straight!"

This sums the situation up for me. Military service should be about behavior and performance and that's it. There must be a very clear code of behavior in the military and anyone—heterosexual or homosexual—who behaves improperly should be thrown out. Period! And where is there a better place to have an enforceable clear code of conduct if not in the military?

Soon after the issue was raised by the President, my colleagues in the Senate were discussing it frankly. There were about 30 of us.

One male Senator gave an impassioned presentation about life in the military: the discipline, the danger, the fear in combat, the importance of your buddy who is next to you in the foxhole with bullets flying over your head—your buddy who could save your life.

His speech was given with tremendous feeling, but as he went on and on, he never made the point about how your buddy's sexual orientation made a difference, how it made him less likely to save you or you, him.

At about five minutes into his talk, the women began to look at each other. The unspoken thought was, "So get to the point—how does sexual orientation fit into what you're talking about?" The male Senators, on the other hand, seemed totally transfixed. Finally, I leaned over to one of them and whispered, "This was good but what does it have to do with gays in the military?" He reprimanded me for "not getting it."

At the end of our colleague's presentation, a female Senator stood up and spoke for the Democratic women by asking a simple question: "Can someone tell me what the problem is here?" From the look on the male faces you would have thought that she had challenged them to a duel at dusk! Mutterings abounded.

A Basic Outlook

I think Democratic women Senators understand that gay or straight, we are all God's children. A basic outlook.

We also understand that mistakes should be learned from, not repeated. When the request for the latest no-strings-attached payment for the Resolution Trust Corporation's savings and loan bailout hit the Senate Banking Committee, it almost flew right through the committee, as if nothing had ever been wrong with the S & Ls.

Patty Murray, Carol Moseley-Braun and I teamed up with John Kerry, spoke to our Banking Chairman Dan Riegel, and were able to set up accountability for this last payment to reimburse those depositors whose savings were lost. "We're not giving the Resolution Trust Corporation a blank check," the women said.

Don't make the same mistake twice. A basic outlook.

Democratic women know that jobs for our people are a basic, over-riding economic goal. When President Clinton put forward a jobs stimulus bill to counteract the effects of the deficit reduction program to come, it was the Democratic women who stood on the Senate floor all through the Senate filibuster to fight for jobs.

A chance at the American dream. A basic outlook.

Democratic women will fight for equality for all, and especially for the most vulnerable in our society: the children, the elderly, the disabled. They touch our emotions and we're not ashamed of that.

A voice for the voiceless. A basic outlook.

Every Democratic woman is a co-sponsor of the Metzenbaum bill to ban semi-automatic weapons. We understand, of course, that people pull the trigger—but there are too many triggers around.

Guns help people kill people. A basic outlook.

We Democratic women understand that we are in politics for one main reason: to make life better for the people we represent by acting to improve their health care, their environment, and their economic security. We will fight for a woman's right to choose with all our energy because we are personally offended at the idea that government should interfere with this most personal of decisions.

The right of privacy is a fundamental right. A basic outlook.

Clearly, I have a bias in favor of female Democratic Senators. I admit it. I believe the basic outlook we share is good for America. And we don't equivocate on this basic outlook; on the contrary, we fight for it.

Senator Don Riegel, who has been in the Senate for 21 years, sees it this way:

The five Democratic women Senators taken together have already changed the center of gravity in the Democratic caucus and the Senate as a whole. The greatest impact has come, I believe, from presenting a different perspective—putting a more sensitive, human-oriented focus on the real problems facing individuals, families, and our country.

The women marvel at the inefficiency—and are poking and prodding for the kinds of changes that will get us focused faster and with better results. They're here to get something done—and their attitude is causing the Senate to lift its sights and move at a quickening pace.

The diversity these women have brought to the Senate reminds us that a true cross-section of America is not 100 men. Their hopefulness and compassion help humanize the Senate. I hope and believe it is making us a more caring and decent institution. I know we are listening better—to new voices that bring the perspective of that vital half of our population that has heretofore been missing.

One recent illustration was Carol Moseley-Braun, who confronted with passion, dignity and great force a misguided effort by Jesse Helms to give official Senate sanction to a Confederate flag emblem. Speaking as the descendent of slaves, she directly challenged what she considered a mistaken Senate vote. Her voice strong with emotion, she asked her colleagues to understand the awful pain it would cause people of color.

It was a transforming event. It triggered an outpouring of support as she cut straight through to the conscience of members, making them hear and think and comprehend in a new way. Senator Campbell of Colorado, a Native American, rose to join her. And then Senator Heflin of Alabama spoke movingly of his Confederate ancestors and said he was changing his vote. It was an electric moment.

At that point Senator Bennett, a much-respected Republican from Utah, announced he was changing his vote, too. Senator Moseley-Braun had rallied Senate members to listen to their better angels. Helms, sputtering his objections, was vanquished. The vote was reversed, and by an overwhelming margin. The Senate as a body had moved itself to higher ground—and it had been led there by a first-term woman Senator.

Riegel says that "while Barbara Mikulski opened the door" by becoming one of the most effective Senators—male or female—"it was Boxer, Feinstein, Moseley-Braun and Murray, who arrived together in 1992, who took the door off its hinges forever."

Clearly, this senior Senator knows the value of women in the Senate.

The 50 Percent Solution

If you agree with me that our country would be a better place with more than five Democratic women in the Senate, I hope you will join me in enacting my "50 Percent Solution"—my plan to see women enter the Senate in numbers reflecting their share of the population.

While I feel very strongly about the need for the 50 Percent Solution, only you can make it happen. Democracy is a living, vibrant system and will reach its zenith only if all of us get involved. From personal experience, I can tell you that you will find it rewarding and fun. You will meet wonderful people who share many of your viewpoints. And you will learn a great deal.

Two organizations are making a tremendous difference—the Democratic Senatorial Campaign Committee Women's Council and EMILY's List. Senator Mikulski and I are co-chairs of the Women's Council of the DSCC.

For the '94 elections the Women's Council's slogan is "Double the score in '94." Whether we can do that depends on a number of factors: the quality of the candidates we attract, the amount of money we can help raise for those candidates, the quality of the campaigns run, the image of the campaigns, and the continued desire of voters for change. It will depend, in addition, on the ability of organizations like the Women's Council and EMILY's List, as well as non-partisan groups like the National Women's Political Caucus, the National Organization for Women, and the Woman's Campaign Fund, to attract and retain enthusiastic donors and volunteers.

The Women's Council has two very clear goals:

- To develop a strong, highly visible network of women donors to the Democratic Senatorial Campaign Committee dedicated to electing Democratic women to the Senate.
- To integrate women into the leadership of the Democratic Party, thus giving them the ability to engage in a direct dialogue with national elected and appointed leadership.

We want not only to encourage women to form a network to help female candidates who have been historically shut out of insider contributions, but to encourage women to become involved in the issues of our day.

The Problem of Money

Raising money for political campaigns is a nightmare; I know it was a personal nightmare for me. I believe it is bad for our country to have candidates for public office spend so much time asking for dollars. In my own campaign, there were days that I felt physically ill at the thought of making one more phone call for money. That's why I have done two things: fought for campaign financing reform and sought a leadership position in the Women's Council.

I fought for campaign finance reform on the floor of the Senate, including getting all the campaign money out of general elections, and setting tough spending limits. Our approach would duplicate what we have done with the Presidential races. With funding provided through a voluntary check off on income tax returns, the Presidential candidates are free to concentrate on their issues and their campaigns in the general election. In other words, there is no private funding needed in the general election, so that incumbents are free to do what they are supposed to do. We also added an excellent funding mechanism—a tax on lobbyists—to ensure there would be enough funding.

Not surprisingly, the move to adopt the Presidential system for funding Senate races failed. In the present Senate, too many like the status quo—incumbents who feel the present nightmare of raising money works to their advantage. They may have given other reasons, and those may have been heartfelt, but when they were all stripped away, the advantages of incumbency tipped the balance.

Thus, my other tack—becoming co-chair of the Women's Council—became even more important, because it allows me to help women candidates and to free them of some of the money-raising torture I went through.

The Women's Council is able to raise funds throughout the country and present them to our Democratic female

Senate nominees after they have won their primaries. The maximum amounts are set by law, in accordance with a state's population.

The Republican Senatorial Campaign Committee can give their candidates the same amounts.

The Women's Council seeks donors of all levels, but the stress is on larger donations—from $1500 up—as the fund-raising goals are mammoth. Fund-raising events priced at $100 and higher are scheduled all over the country. Smaller donations are solicited by mail.

The Power of Early Money: EMILY's List

EMILY's List is the biggest fund-raising organization for women in the country. Every Democratic woman in the United States Senate credits EMILY's List for a large part of her success.

Important as the money is, it isn't only the dollars but the enthusiasm of those who participate. There, members of EMILY's List stand in a class by themselves.

Founded by Ellen Malcolm in 1985, EMILY's List stands for *Early Money Is Like Yeast*. "Yeast makes the dough rise," says Malcolm with a grin, over and over again, all across the country—where chapters of EMILY's List are popping up like mushrooms after rain.

Early money is key because one of the elements of electoral success is defining one's own campaign and oneself. If you don't have funding to get out there and do that, you can bet your opponent will—and it won't be pretty. It also won't be true, but that's the nature of the campaign beast we have created.

What has been remarkable about EMILY's List is that Ellen and her organization have tapped into a source no one thought was there. Veteran fund-raiser and political advisor Bob Burkette of California put it this way to the

Congressional Quarterly on October 17, 1992—before the November election: "Emily has loosened up a universe of donors that didn't give in the past."

EMILY's List raises money through networking—women telling women, telling women. That's how it started. Ellen Malcolm says she started with her rolodex and then her friends brought out their rolodexes—and from there, it all snowballed.

In 1986, EMILY contributed $350,000 to endorsed candidates; in 1992, EMILY contributed over $6,000,000 to endorsed candidates. This was a revolution—women writing checks to women, shattering all the myths of the '50s.

When you join EMILY's List for $100 on up, you also pledge to assist at least three of their endorsed female candidates during the year. You send your checks to Malcolm's office in Washington, D.C. Your contribution is recorded and sent on to the candidates you designate.

Why EMILY's List is Different

Some in the Senate and House are trying to do away with EMILY's List because the organization "bundles" checks and presents them to the candidates, much the way corporate political action committees (PACs) do. My belief is that EMILY's List is one of the healthiest things to happen to politics in a long time, awakening people who have never participated, making our democracy vibrant. These new contributors have no special economic interest and yet they are compared to corporate executives with special economic interests who "bundle" for candidates' contributions. To my mind, the two are not comparable.

During the debates of 1993 on campaign reform, the *Los Angeles Times* printed a sharply critical story about the support for EMILY's List by women members of Congress who consider themselves agents of change, as if the women were protecting "politics as unusual." I thought the *Times* story stood logic on its head. EMILY's List *is* change.

I submitted an op-ed piece to the *Los Angeles Times* rebutting their story, but they chose not to run it. In this piece, you'll find my admiration for EMILY's List and my commitment to seeing it survive so that the political revolution of women can continue.

My piece read as follows:

> I wasn't the insiders' choice for the Senate seat I currently hold. I didn't get the "smart" money or the high donors who flock to front runners. When I declared my candidacy, the political pundits predicted I couldn't raise the money. They said I didn't even have a chance. But, last November the people of California proved them wrong.
>
> My experience demonstrates the need for real political finance reform. I know the deck is stacked, because it was stacked against me. I couldn't get elected the "traditional" way; I had to build my campaign around a grassroots participation, a broad base of low-dollar donors, and support from people previously uninvolved in the process.
>
> Real political reform should open up the system to those candidates who have been shut out. And that's what EMILY's List does. Unfortunately, in the recent debate over the "bundling" provisions of Campaign Finance Reform, those facts have gotten lost. An article that appeared in last Friday's edition of the *Los Angeles Times* implied that Barbara Boxer and Dianne Feinstein's support for groups like EMILY's List was actually a cynical attempt to

preserve the status quo. Nothing could be further from the truth.

Throughout my entire career I have fought to reform our campaign finance system. I believe that the proposal currently being debated in the U.S. Senate represents real reform. It would help take the special interest money out of politics by banning PACs, prohibiting contributions by lobbyists, and creating a system—funded by a tax on lobbyists— that limits campaign expenditures. These reforms take power away from the well-heeled Washington insiders and place it in the hands of the American people.

I am speaking out because I know that the last time the Congress passed legislation to reform campaign financing, the experience of elected women was not considered. The result? Women actually lost ground. After the 1974 reform bill was enacted, we lost Democratic women in the House, and elected no Democratic women to the Senate. Only after EMILY's List was founded in 1985 did we begin to turn those numbers around.

But the numbers tell only half the story. The truth is that in just five months, the women Senators have shaken up the Senate and made a real difference . . .

In these Senate debates, we have offered a new perspective. We have made a real difference. But there's still much more to do.

Grassroots organizations like EMILY's List are not the problem; they are part of the solution. EMILY's List does not lobby and has no economic interest in the outcome of elections. Since its founding, thousands of men and women have joined EMILY's List because they believe we need to elect more women candidates. The begin by writing $100 checks to the candidate of their choice. With non-incumbents receiving 98 percent of these contributions, EMILY's List has helped bring new perspectives to the U.S. Congress.

We need to make sure that the support EMILY's List provided us will be there for the next generation of female candidates. What is at stake is not the future of Barbara Boxer or Dianne Feinstein, but the future of women candidates yet to come.

The reform I support is one that works to change the face of the United States Senate, reform that served to mobilize thousands of women and others previously uninvolved in the political process, and reform that will open up the doors of the Congress to women candidates from every city and every state of this nation. We should not slam the door on them.

By the way, Republican women have started their version of EMILY's list, called WISH, for Women in the Senate and House.

With the permission of the Center for the American Woman and Politics, I am reprinting, in the *Appendix* of this book, their list of organizations that gave campaign contributions to women and their 1992 activities. The center asks that you contact them if you know of such a national organization that is not on their list.

Status Quo Politics or the 50 Percent Solution

The policies made in the United States Senate effect everything about our lives: war and peace, a sound economy, clean air and water, health research and reform, the status of our children, human and civil rights, education, the right to choose, government spending priorities. Everything about our lives.

If you feel that for government to be meaningful to all our people, it should be representative of all our people, then don't sit on the sidelines. Whether you are working in the workplace or at home, get off the sidelines; whether you are a nurse or a computer operator, get off the sidelines; whether you are a student or a doctor or a truck driver or an automechanic, get off the sidelines.

Remember, those who like the status quo hope you'll stay there. Don't let them win. Don't let them keep us as Strangers in the Senate.

Afterword

To Those Who Take the Risk

As you have seen, I would not have become a United States Senator without the love and support of family, friends, colleagues, and thousands of people who believed in me.

I believe the experiences I have had in politics are not that different from the personal challenges people face in their lives.

The following is a very special letter written by a dear friend, Paul Littman. It was sent to me when things were rough. I reprint it here with the hope that it will inspire you to follow your dreams.

Dear Barbara,

As all letters start, I hope you are feeling well. I know at this time you are riding an emotional roller coaster. For you this must be more difficult than it is for most of us. So much of what you project is dependent on your positive and sincere emotions. People who are fortunate enough to spend time with you cannot help but react to your spiritual intelligence. You are an inspiration to all who come in contact with you. This race you are engaged in is not just for you. It's for all of us who you inspire. And it is not just about winning, but the attempt. It's a great burden to carry the thoughts and aspirations of other people, but you represent what we hold true and dear. You have always dreamed the impossible dream and it is your effort to reach the unreachable stars that we draw inspiration from.

There comes a time in every marathon that the runner suddenly feels fatigued and lonely. In spite of thousands of people who line the street cheering him on. He will feel this loneliness and isolation. It is at this point that he confronts himself. He is the only one who will ever know if he gave his best or not. He must find the courage and determination to go on. The marathon runner represents all those who stand and cheer.

I hope you will find the resources within yourself to overcome the unexpected obstacles. I hope you will not allow your spirit to be diminished.

I know you will always be an inspiration to those of us who love you.

Paul

Appendix

Center to Prevent Handgun Violence
1225 "I" Street, N.W.
Washington, D.C. 20055
(202) 289-7314

The John and Michelle Scully Fund
of the San Francisco Foundation
685 Market Street
Suite 910
San Francisco, CA 94105
****

From the **Center for the American Woman and Politics:**
Eagleton Institute of Politics, Rutgers University
New Brunswick, NJ 08901
(908) 828-2210

Ain't I A Woman Network/PAC (Philadelphia, Penn.)
Alabama Solution (Birmingham, Al.)
Arkansas Women's Action Fund (Little Rock, Ark.)
Committee of 21 (New Orleans, La.)
The Committee for the Election of Western New York Women
   (Buffalo, N.Y.)
Eleanor Roosevelt Fund of California (Sunnyvail, Calif.)
EMILY's List (Washington, D.C.)
Hollywood Women's Political Committee (Culver City, Calif.)
H.O.P.E. Chest (Mobile, Al.)
The Hope Chest (Columbus, Ohio)

HOPE-PAC (Los Angeles, Calif.)
Kathleen Recommends (Los Angeles, Calif.)
Latina PAC (Sacramento, Calif.)
The Leader PAC (Fairfax Station, Va.)
Los Angeles African American Women's PAC
   (Los Angeles, Calif.)
Los Angeles Women's Campaign Fund (Sherman Oaks, Calif.)
Marin County Women's PAC (Tiburon, Calif.)
Michigan Women's Campaign Fund (Troy, Mich.)
Minnesota Women's Campaign Fund (St. Paul, Minn.)
Missouri Women's Action Fund (St. Louis, Mo.)
National Federation of Business & Professional Women's Clubs
   (BPW/PAC)
National Organization for Women PAC (Washington, D.C.)
National Women's Political Caucus (Washington, D.C.)
Pennsylvania Women's Campaign Fund (Avondale, Pa.)
Republican Women's PAC—*currently inactive* (Sacramento, Calif.)
Sacramento Women's Campaign Fund (Sacramento, Calif.)
Santa Barbara Women's Political Committee (Santa Barbara, Calif.)
Task Force 2000 PAC (Houston, Texas)
Wednesday Committee (Los Angeles, Calif.)
WISH List (Red Bank, N.J.)
Women For: (Beverly Hills, Calif.)
Women For: Orange County (Irvine, Calif.)
Women in Illinois Needed Now (WIINN) (Rockford, Ill.)
Women in Psychology for Legislative Action (Roslindale, Mass.)
Women in the Nineties (WIN) (Nashville, Tenn.)
Women Organizing Women PAC (WOW PAC) (New Haven, Conn.)
Women's Campaign Fund (Washington, D.C.)
Women's Council of the Democratic Senatorial Campaign Committee
   (Washington, D.C.)
Women's Investment Network (WIN-PAC) (Portland, Ore.)
Women's Political Action Commitee of N.J. (Edison, N.J.)
Women's Political Committee (Los Angeles, Calif.)
Women's Political Fund (San Francisco, Calif.)

Index